Madagascar:

Malaria Operational Plan FY 2014

TABLE OF CONTENTS

ACRONYMS AND ABBREVIATIONS

ACT	artemisinin-based combination therapy
AMFm	Affordable Medicines Facility – malaria
AMM	*Agence de Médicament de Madagascar*
ANC	antenatal care
AS/AQ	artesunate-amodiaquine
BEST	best practices at scale in the home, community and facilities
BCC	behavioral change communication
CDC	Centers for Disease Control and Prevention
CDS	Comité de Développement Sanitaire /*Health Development Committee*
CHL	central highlands
CHW	community health worker
CRR	country results review
CSB	*centre de santé de base*
DFID	Department for International Development
DHS	Demographic and Health Survey
EPI	expanded program on immunization
FBO	faith based organization
FIND	Foundation for Innovative new Diagnostics
Global Fund	Global Fund to Fight AIDS, Tuberculosis and Malaria
GHI	Global Health Initiative
GoM	Government of Madagascar
HIV	human immunodeficiency virus
HMIS	health management information system
HSS	health systems strengthening
iCCM	integrated community case management
IPM	*Institut Pasteur de Madagascar*
IPR	implementation and procurement reform
IPTp	intermittent preventive treatment for pregnant women
IRS	indoor residual spraying
ITN	insecticide-treated net
IVM	integrated vector management
LLIN	long-lasting insecticide-treated net
MDG	Millennium Development Goal
MIP	malaria in pregnancy
MIS	malaria indicator survey
MoH	Ministry of Health
MOP	malaria operational plan
NMCP	National Malaria Control Program
NGO	non-governmental organization
NTDs	neglected tropical diseases
OP	organophosphate
PCV	Peace Corps Volunteer
PEPFAR	President's Emergency Plan for AIDS Relief
PhaGDis	*Pharmacie de Gros de District* (District pharmaceutical depots)

PLWHA	people living with HIV/AIDS
PMI	President's Malaria Initiative
PR	principal recipient
RA	resident advisor
RBM	Roll Back Malaria
RDT	rapid diagnostic test
SALAMA	Madagascar central medical stores
SP	sulfadoxine-pyrimethamine
SSD	*service de santé de district*
UNICEF	United Nations Children's Fund
USAID	United States Agency for International Development
USG	United States Government
WHO	World Health Organization
WHOPES	WHO Pesticide Evaluation Scheme

I. EXECUTIVE SUMMARY

Malaria prevention and control are major foreign assistance objectives of the U.S. Government (USG). In May 2009, President Barack Obama announced the Global Health Initiative (GHI), a comprehensive effort to reduce the burden of disease and promote healthy communities and families around the world. Through the GHI, the United States will help partner countries improve health outcomes, with a particular focus on improving the health of women, newborns, and children.

The President's Malaria Initiative (PMI) is a core component of GHI, along with HIV/AIDS and tuberculosis programs. PMI was launched in June 2005 as a 5-year, $1.2 billion initiative to rapidly scale up malaria prevention and treatment interventions and reduce malaria-related mortality by 50% in 15 high-burden countries in sub-Saharan Africa by 2010. With passage of the 2008 Lantos-Hyde Act, funding for PMI was extended and, as part of the GHI, the goal of PMI was adjusted to reduce malaria-related mortality by 70% in the original 15 countries by the end of 2015. Programming of PMI activities follows the core principles of GHI: encouraging country ownership and investing in country-led plans and health systems; increasing impact and efficiency through strategic coordination and programmatic integration; strengthening and leveraging key partnerships, multilateral organizations, and private contributions; implementing a woman- and girl-centered approach; improving monitoring and evaluation; and promoting research and innovation.

Madagascar was in the third wave of eight new PMI countries in 2008 which brought the total to 15 focus countries. Full implementation began in Madagascar with FY 2008 funding. Malaria is a major health problem in Madagascar, although its epidemiology varies considerably in different regions of the country. On the East Coast transmission is stable and perennial, while the West Coast has a long, rainy transmission season and a brief dry season. Almost one-third of the Central Highlands is above 1,500 meters elevation, where malaria transmission rarely occurs. In the rest of the Central Highlands, however, transmission is seasonal and moderately unstable with occasional epidemics. The semi-desert South has highly seasonal and unstable transmission and is also vulnerable to epidemics. In the most recent large-scale epidemic in the Central Highlands in the late 1980s, an estimated 30,000 people died.

Madagascar has been the recipient of eight malaria grants from the Global Fund to Fight AIDS, Tuberculosis and Malaria (Global Fund). The current grants under implementation are: a $64 million Rolling Continuation Channel 4 grant signed in October 2009; a $48.7 Round 7 malaria grant ending in September 2013, and a Round 9 National Strategy Application (NSA) II that should be signed in June 2013. The United Nations Children's Fund (UNICEF) has played a major role in the prevention and treatment of malaria during pregnancy; the distribution of insecticide-treated nets (ITNs); and the implementation of integrated community case management of malaria, pneumonia, and diarrheal diseases in children under five at the community level. The World Health Organization, the Clinton Foundation, and the Principality of Monaco have been important sources of technical assistance to the *Programme National de Lutte Contre le Paludisme* (National Malaria Control Program; NMCP).

Following the political crisis and *coup d'état* in March 2009, all U. S. Government support to the current government, from the central level to the primary care health facility level, was suspended. The suspension will remain in effect until a freely and fairly elected government is in place. This FY 2014 Malaria Operational Plan was developed based on the assumption that U.S. Government suspensions will remain in place. Planning for FY 2014 was carried out in Madagascar in March 2013 and included representatives from the United States Agency for International Development and the United States Centers for Disease Control and Prevention staff based in Washington, Atlanta, and Madagascar. The planning team met with implementing and international partners to better coordinate PMI activities; the team also met with NMCP and other Government of Madagascar personnel. The proposed FY 2014 PMI budget for Madagascar is $25.92 million.

The suspension of all activities that require direct collaboration with the Government has impeded full application of the fundamental tenets of the GHI. Nevertheless, over the past four years, PMI has focused support on the Madagascar National Strategic Plan for malaria; increased efficiencies through greater coordination and programmatic integration with key partners; implemented woman- and girl-centered approaches through its community-level programming; and improved and expanded the monitoring and evaluation of the program. The following major activities will be supported with FY 2014 funding:

Insecticide-treated nets (ITNs): PMI is supporting the Madagascar National Strategic Plan 2013-17 goal of universal coverage with 1 long-lasting ITN per 2 persons in 93 of the 112 health districts where seasonal or perennial malaria transmission occurs. PMI supports free mass distribution campaigns to achieve equitable coverage, and will support keep-up strategies, such as continuous distribution methods at the community level to replace expired nets and to reach pregnant women, based on the results of a 12-month pilot continuous distribution that starts in July 2013. PMI also supports distribution of replacement ITNs after natural disasters such as cyclones in affected areas and supports social marketing of highly subsidized ITNs in limited peri-urban areas.

PMI supported the first rolling mass ITN distribution campaign from November 2009 to November 2010 and contributed 3.6 million free long-lasting ITNs representing 49% of the nets distributed. By 2011, household ownership of at least one ITN had increased to over 94% and ITN use to 82% in targeted zones. However, the average number of ITNs per household was 1.8, falling short of the previous national goal of two per household (Malaria Indicator Survey 2011). With FY 2011 and FY 2012 funding, PMI procured approximately 4.8 million ITNs (45%) of the 10.2 million planned for free distribution in the 2012/2013 campaign to replace ITNs distributed in 2009/2010. With FY 2013 funds, PMI will procure approximately 1.45 million ITNs for community-based continuous distribution. A portion of these net will be used as needed to respond to cyclones and malaria epidemics.

With FY 2014 funding, PMI will procure approximately 2.8 million ITNs for distribution during the 2015 mass distribution campaign, which will replace part of the ITNs distributed during 2012/2013.

Indoor residual spraying (IRS): The 2011 Malaria Indicator Survey (MIS) showed 79% of households in the 53 districts that received blanket IRS in 2010 reported being sprayed sometime during the 12 months preceding the survey, and 82% of children under five years of age, 78% of pregnant women, and 82% of all individuals in the IRS-targeted districts reported sleeping in households protected by IRS. The 2013–2017 National Malaria Strategy calls for focalized IRS stratified at the commune level in the Central Highlands (CHL), Fringe, and South and West extension zones previously covered by three to four years of blanket spraying. The strategy calls for focalized IRS in 2014, covering up to 30% of communes in previously sprayed zones and prioritizing those at high-risk, identified using clinical case data with evidence of the highest transmission. Spraying will be coupled with surveillance to ensure rapid detection and response to malaria outbreaks. With FY 2012 funds, PMI-supported IRS sprayed about 330,000 structures and protected approximately 1.6 million people in 15 districts in the Central Highlands, Fringe and the South.

With FY 2014 funds, and in coordination with Global Fund-supported IRS activities, PMI will support targeted IRS in 15 districts in the Central Highlands, Fringe, and the South, spraying approximately 396,000 structures. PMI will also continue its environmental mitigation measures, improve monitoring and supervision, as well as expand its support for entomologic monitoring and evaluation.

Malaria in Pregnancy (MIP): Intermittent preventive treatment in pregnancy (IPTp) using sulfadoxine-pyrimethamine (SP) was adopted as a national policy in late 2004 in the 93 districts where stable malaria transmission occurs. The 2008/2009 Demographic Health Survey (DHS) showed that 86% of pregnant women reported making at least one antenatal care (ANC) visit. Despite this high rate of ANC attendance, the percentage of women in zones who reported receiving at least one dose of sulfadoxine-pyrimethamine during an ANC clinic visit was only 15%, while only 8% reported receiving two or more doses (DHS 2008-2009). These figures increased to 31% and 22%, respectively by 2011 (MIS 2011). The causes for the poor uptake of IPTp are unclear. Because of the political constraints related to working with Government of Madagascar since March 2009, PMI has focused its efforts to prevent and control malaria in pregnancy on behavior change communication (BCC) at the community level to promote early and frequent ANC clinic attendance and improve understanding of the benefits of IPTp. With FY 2014 funding, PMI will continue to support client-targeted BCC, focusing on malaria in pregnancy services using trained community health workers (CHWs). PMI will coordinate with the NMCP, the Directorate of Child and Maternal Health, and Reproductive Health and partners, to link malaria interventions for pregnant women with integrated antenatal health services. PMI will also procure SP for distribution via nongovernmental organizations (NGO) and faith-based organizations (FBO), and approximately 3 million tablets of combination iron/low-dose folic acid supplements for distribution via CHWs to pregnant women as an integral part of prenatal care.

Case management: Results from the 2011 MIS show that among children under five with fever in the two weeks preceding the survey, only 41% sought any kind of treatment and only 3.1% were treated with an artemisinin-based combination therapy (ACT) within 24 hours of fever onset. The NMCP policy requires that, where possible, all cases of malaria be diagnosed by microscopy or a rapid diagnostic test (RDT). PMI activities to improve diagnostics, supply chain management, and case management at public health facilities were suspended in FY 2009. While working under political restriction since that time, PMI has invested in community-based interventions, and support to private sector NGOs and FBOs. PMI has supported integrated community case management (iCCM) of malaria, pneumonia, and diarrhea in rural communities more than five kilometers from the nearest health facility and has reached about one-third of those communities nationwide. To date, PMI has supported training of more than 8,500 CHWs in malaria case management including use of RDTs for diagnosis. PMI has also supported training in malaria diagnostics and RDT use of 176 providers from 147 NGO &FBO run health facilities, In addition PMI supported the training of supervisors in malaria microscopy diagnosis in 48 health facilities. In collaboration with implementing partners, PMI has set up 933 malaria commodities supply points at the commune level to serve the CHWs.

With FY 2014 funding, PMI will strengthen the supply chain for CHWs and procure sufficient RDTs to fill the gap nationally for community case management of malaria. PMI will also ensure the supply of RDTs to approximately 300 clinics run by nongovernmental and faith-based organizations. All ACT needs are expected to be filled by Global Fund grants. PMI will continue its support to the network of CHWs for the use of ACTs and RDTs at the community level and CHW training for integrated case management of malaria, pneumonia, and diarrheal diseases.

Behavior Change Communication (BCC): PMI supports a variety of BCC strategies to promote healthy behaviors including mass- and mid-media approaches such as radio spots, mobile videos with local actors, and print materials for sensitization. PMI continues its support for the *Champion Commune* approach, which works with the local Health Development committees (CDS), NGOs, and Roll Back Malaria partners to establish an innovative community empowerment and mobilization program. Through the SanteNet2 project, the approach allowed CDS members to establish and support a network of community health workers, within the larger context communal development.

In FY 2014, PMI will coordinate with the NMCP and partners to strengthen BCC approaches for malaria prevention and treatment at the community level by emphasizing interpersonal communication methods as the majority of BCC investment. This will include the promotion of the *Champion Commune* approach, with a particular focus on an integrated community management of pneumonia, diarrheal diseases, and malaria. PMI will be a major contributor to BCC activities supporting the national ITN and IRS campaigns. PMI will also collaborate with the Peace Corps on activities to improve malaria treatment-seeking and prevention behaviors.

Monitoring and evaluation (M&E): The NMCP, Global Fund, and other partners, has developed a National Malaria M&E Strategy and Plan. PMI contributed to the nationwide 2008/2009 DHS, the 2011 and 2013 MIS, the 2013 Millennium Development Goal survey and continues to provide support for fever surveillance at 15 sentinel sites. PMI is working with partners to strengthen M&E for community-based interventions.

With FY 2014 funding, PMI will strengthen M&E nationally by supporting expansion, improving reporting quality, and ensuring timeliness of epidemic surveillance. PMI will support the planning and implementation for the next MIS, including the collection of malaria biomarkers, slated for 2015. PMI will also continue to support high-quality data reporting of malaria indicators from the 15 fever sentinel sites and 10 entomology monitoring sites.

II. STRATEGY

1. Introduction

The President's Malaria Initiative (PMI) is a core component of the GHI to achieve improvements in health outcomes and health-related Millennium Development Goals. PMI was launched in June 2005 as a five-year, $1.2 billion initiative to rapidly scale up malaria prevention and treatment interventions and reduce malaria-related mortality by 50% in 15 high-burden countries in sub-Saharan Africa. With passage of the 2008 Lantos-Hyde Act, funding for PMI was extended and, as part of the GHI, the goal of PMI was adjusted to reduce malaria-related mortality by 70% in the original 15 countries by the end of 2015. This will be achieved by continuing to scale up coverage of proven preventive and therapeutic interventions, including insecticide-treated nets (ITNs), indoor residual spraying (IRS), intermittent preventive treatment of pregnant women (IPTp), and artemisinin-based combination therapies (ACTs).

FY 2008 was the first year of PMI funding in Madagascar. The FY 2014 Malaria Operational Plan presents a detailed implementation plan for Madagascar based on the National Malaria Control Program's (NMCP's) five-year National Strategic Plan, 2013-2017. The activities that PMI is proposing to support fit in well with the 2013–2017 National Malaria Control Strategy and build on investments made by PMI and other partners, including the Global Fund to Fight AIDS, Tuberculosis, and Malaria (Global Fund), to improve and expand malaria-related services. This document briefly reviews the current status of malaria control policies and interventions in Madagascar, describes progress to date, identifies challenges and unmet needs if the targets of the NMCP and PMI are to be achieved, and provides a description of planned FY 2014 activities.

FY 2014 MOP assumes that suspension of United States Government (USG) assistance will remain, limiting PMI's technical assistance and development interventions.

2. Malaria Situation in Madagascar

The estimated population of Madagascar is 22.6 million of which approximately 19% are children under five years of age and 4.5 % are pregnant women. Madagascar is one of the poorest countries in the world with an average per capita income of $430[1]; 77% of the population live under the poverty line, an increase from 69% in 2011[2]. In 2011, malaria was the second leading cause of death among children under five reported from district hospitals.[3] Life expectancy is 64 years for women and 61 years for men.

Madagascar witnessed a decade of health improvement between 1997 and 2008. According to the 2008/2009 Demographic and Health Survey (DHS), infant and child mortality fell from 159 per 1,000 live births in 1997 to 72 per 1,000 live births by 2008. Other determinants of child

---

[1] World Bank, 2011
[2] EPM 2005, EPM 2010
[3,3] Annuaire Statistique 2010

survival–such as morbidity and coverage of important health interventions–have improved significantly during this period. For instance, between 1997 and 2008, the prevalence of diarrhea in children decreased by about 70% and respiratory infections by approximately 87%, while the proportion of moderately or severely anemic children fell 59% between 1997 and 2008.

Despite recent improvements in child health indicators, Madagascar still faces major health challenges, which threaten social and economic development. Access to and quality of health services have been negatively impacted by the political crisis, which started with the March 2009 coup and led to more than 200 *centre de santé de base* (CSB) closures over the last four years. National health infrastructure, information, and commodity management systems are extremely weak, and much remains to be done at central and regional levels to ensure quality services and sustainable health financing.

These challenges have a significant impact on overall health and malaria activities at every level of the public health system. There have been delays in planned health policy reform, limited supervisory and monitoring visits due to security issues and lack of funds, delayed data reporting, and interruptions in supplies of essential medicines to the health facility level. The nongovernmental sector has reported difficulties due to insecurity in the field and reduced capacity of the health sector at the decentralized level as a result of changes in personnel and delays in fund disbursements.

Malaria transmission and epidemiology: Malaria is endemic in 90% of Madagascar; however the entire population is considered to be at risk for the disease. Malaria cases and deaths reported through the national Health Management Information System (HMIS) have fallen between 2003 and 2011. Overall, hospital deaths attributed to malaria fell from 17% in 2003 to 7% in 2011. In 2012, malaria was the fourth leading cause of outpatient consultation, [4] and 5% of all children under five years of age admitted to a hospital were diagnosed with severe malaria. Severe malaria remained among the top five causes of reported overall mortality.

The country has been stratified into four malaria epidemiologic zones based on the duration and intensity of malaria transmission: the West Coast including the North; the Central Highlands; the East Coast; and the South, roughly corresponding to the bioclimate map below. The rainy season varies, starting in late October or early November and lasts until April or May; however, on the East Coast the rainy season and increased malaria transmission may last as long as nine months. The cyclone season extends from December to April. In February 2013, Cyclone Haruna hit Madagascar, resulting in widespread devastation and destruction of homes and property in the southwest. Cyclones often result in flooding and increased risk of communicable diseases and malaria, compounded by the loss of ITNs.

---

[4] Annuaire Statistique, 2012 (to be released June2013)

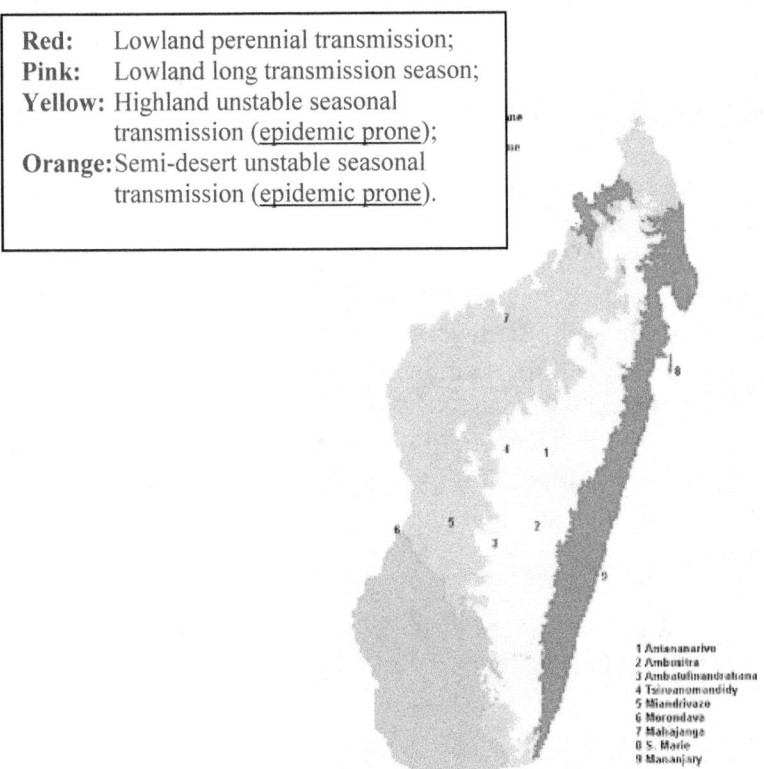

Red: Lowland perennial transmission;
Pink: Lowland long transmission season;
Yellow: Highland unstable seasonal transmission (<u>epidemic prone</u>);
Orange: Semi-desert unstable seasonal transmission (<u>epidemic prone</u>).

1 Antananarivo
2 Ambositra
3 Ambatofinandrahana
4 Tsiroanomandidy
5 Miandrivazo
6 Morondava
7 Mahajanga
8 S. Marie
9 Mananjary

The East Coast has perennial transmission and the West Coast has seasonal transmission that typically runs from May to October with reduced transmission in July and August. In both regions, immunity among adults is reported to be high and most morbidity and mortality is among children under five and pregnant women. Almost one-third of the Central Highlands lies above 1,500 meters, where malaria transmission does not occur, or the transmission season is short, seasonal, and unstable. In the semi-desert South, transmission is also seasonal but very unstable and in some areas, is almost absent. Immunity is limited in the human population of both the upper Central Highlands and the South, and those areas are prone to periodic epidemics, which are often associated with high levels of mortality in all age groups. The most recent large-scale epidemic occurred in the late 1980s in the Central Highlands and killed an estimated 30,000 people. The Fringe districts of the Central Highlands are those areas with an altitude between 800 and 900 meters that lie between the epidemic-prone areas of upper Central Highlands and the malaria-endemic areas on the coasts.

Because of the scale-up of prevention and case management interventions over the past few years, the transmission dynamics of malaria are changing. The new national strategy has organized the country into three geographic zones based on the local epidemiology and level of coverage of malaria interventions: control, consolidation, and pre-elimination zones.[5]

---

[5] WHO *Malaria Elimination: A field manual for low and moderate endemic countries*

11

While *Plasmodium falciparum* is the predominant species of malaria parasite in all areas, *P. vivax*, *P. malariae*, and *P. ovale* together may make up as much as 10-15% of all cases, especially in the Highlands. The two primary vectors are *Anopheles gambiae* (East and West Coasts) and *An. funestus* (Central Highlands and South). *An. arabiensis* is present in all four epidemiological zones. *An. funestus* increases in abundance during the rice-growing season and was the primary vector responsible for the outbreaks in the Central Highlands in the late 1980s. Since this vector prefers to feed and rest indoors, it is quite sensitive to IRS. *An. arabiensis,* also present in the Central Highlands, is more ecologically independent of humans and their domestic environment. *An. mascarensis* has been reported as a primary vector in the southeast and as a secondary vector on the island district of Sainte Marie.

Following the national scale-up of malaria prevention interventions from 2006 – 2010 and accompanying decline in malaria morbidity, the Malaria Indicator Survey (MIS) conducted from April–May, 2011, during the high transmission season, showed lower than expected parasitemia prevalence among children under five years old. The overall prevalence of malaria parasitemia among children under five was 6% nationally with the following point estimates: 1% in the Central Highlands, 1% in the bordering Fringe zone, 1% in the South, 4% on the West Coast, and 16% on the East Coast as seen in Figure 2.

Figure 2: Malaria parasitemia in children less than 5 years of age, Madagascar, 2011

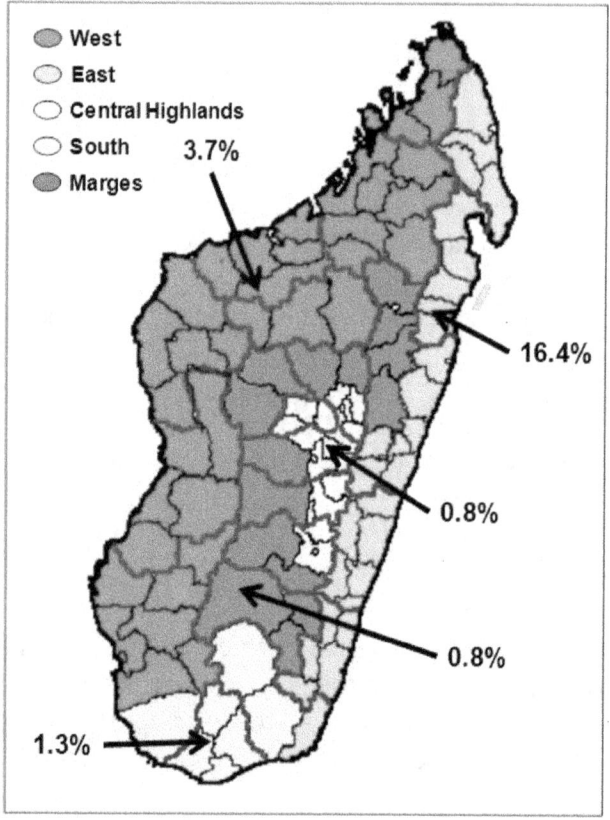

In spite of these gains, epidemics in 2011 and 2012 arising in typically endemic areas where transmission has decreased in recent years underscores the importance of strong surveillance and response systems. These findings suggest that the South East coast is in transition from a typically endemic zone with near year-round transmission to an epidemic-prone zone. Initial findings from an investigation suggest that the combination of decreased malaria immunity and decreased ITN ownership and use rates between 2011 and 2012, just two years after a universal ITN distribution campaign, were among the contributing factors. HMIS data show overall in Madagascar a 180% increase in cases during the first four months of 2012 compared to the same time period in 2011. This underscores the need to maintain high levels of malaria prevention coverage between campaigns and improve access to prompt case management.

3. Country Health System

The MOH at the national level is represented by the cabinet of the minister of health and the national directorates reporting directly to the MOH Director General under the Secretary General of the MOH.

Madagascar is administratively divided into 22 regions, 119 districts and 1,579 communes, and 17,485 fokontany,[6] the equivalent of villages in other African countries. Each region has a regional health directorate and a regional hospital. There are only 112 health districts. Contrary to other administrators in Madagascar the fokontany chief is chosen through a grass roots selection process by community members and is not affiliated with a political party.

The organization of the health system follows the same general organization as the administrative system down to the district level. At the commune level there is at least one public primary health care facility, known as a *centre de santé deb* (CSB), serving each commune. The formal health system is composed of four levels:

- There are eight university teaching hospitals in the capital city and five former provinces that serve as specialized referral centers.
- There are 18 regional hospitals for patients requiring a higher level of care that serve as tertiary care health facilities.
- There are 87 district hospitals that serve as referral facilities (secondary care) for the primary health centers.
- There are over 2,545 public primary health centers or CSB. Among these 1,635 are known as CSB Level II and are supposed to be staffed with at least one doctor. There are also 910 CSB I, staffed by a nurse or paramedic and in some cases a nurse's aide.

In addition, more than 350 health facilities are run by NGO/FBOs. Some FBO-run hospitals are part of the district level hospitals.

The MOH has a critical staff shortage at all levels of the public health system, especially for service provision below the central level. In addition, health workers are not distributed equitably throughout the country, resulting in higher concentrations of qualified health staff in the urban areas. According to the 2011 National Census (Annuaire des Statistiques), the national ratio of

---

[6] INSTAT, 2012

doctors to the population was 1 per 6,925, with rural regions having less than one doctor for every 10,000 inhabitants.

Regional directors oversee health teams that implement integrated health interventions; currently all regional teams and district health teams have malaria focal persons. The District Hospital is the first referral structure for CSBs; the district health team, currently known as *service de santé de district* (SSD) is headed by a medical chief called *Médécin Inspecteur*, responsible for technical supervision of all CSBs in his/her jurisdiction.

The NMCP was established in 1921 with the aim of preventing malaria epidemics. Until the late 1980s, the focus was on the 26 epidemic-prone districts. In 1998, the first five-year national malaria control strategy was designed, defining control interventions per transmission zones and introducing the use of chloroquine for community-based malaria treatment and chemoprophylaxis among pregnant women. In June 2011, the GOM elevated the SLP to a National Malaria Control Program (NMCP) directorate level in the MOH organizational structure. Assisted by a Deputy Director, the NMCP Director supervises a team comprising six technical divisions: Vector Control, Case Management, Laboratory, Epidemiologic Surveillance, M&E, and BCC, and one support division: Finance and Administration.[7]

The non-public health service delivery comprises active participation of the Lutheran, Protestant, and Catholic Churches through over 350 health facilities scattered around the island, varying in size, equipment and staffing. The majority of these facilities are classified as CSBs. In addition, NGOs and private providers run smaller health facilities. In 2012, PMI supported training and donation of malaria commodities, mostly RDTs, in 161 non-public facilities offering malaria diagnostics and treatment services.

In 2008, Madagascar approved an integrated community case management (iCCM) package offered by Community Health Workers to provide health services at the village level. Currently, CHWs provide treatment for uncomplicated malaria with ACTs, acute respiratory infections with antibiotics, diarrhea with oral rehydration solution (ORS) and zinc tablets, family planning for eligible families, micronutrient supplementation, and nutrition monitoring and referral. The community-based health services policy plans that CHWs will provide a more comprehensive package of services including primary care to newborns. A recent pilot intervention testing the resupply of pregnant women in iron and folic acid by CHWs was successful and will be scaled up. Based on the national implementation directives, each fokontany has a team of two CHWs, one specializing in child health and another specializing in maternal and reproductive health. Plans are underway to cross-train all CHWs so that they can at least advise and refer all maternal and child patients in their respective communities. There are over 35,000 CHWs in the country, trained mostly by a Global Fund NSA grant and by USAID-funded bilateral projects.

The iCCM package delivered by CHWs supported by USAID-funded projects targets populations in villages located five kilometers or more than one hour's walk from the nearest health facility. However, the selection and establishment of CHWs supported by the Global Fund is not based on the same distance criteria. Efforts are underway to harmonize the two approaches. In addition, three directorates in the MOH--NMCP, Maternal Child and

---

[7] Plan Strategique National 2013-2017

Reproductive Health (DSEMR), and the Health Districts Directorate (DDS) -- have a share in the oversight of the iCCM activities, which makes coordination and ownership a challenge. Especially challenging are harmonization of supervision tools and content, commodity management, activity reporting and data management.

4. National Malaria Control Plan and Strategy

Madagascar's National Strategic Plan for the period 2013- 2017 identifies different epidemiological levels and provides key intervention for each phase: control, consolidation and pre-elimination. The table below describes the key strategies in each of Madagascar's transmission zones.

Table 1: NMCP Strategy by Intervention and Transmission Zone

Strategies/interventions	Higher-Transmission Control Zones (<80% coverage of interventions: Scale-up)	Moderate to low Transmission (≥ 80% intervention coverage: Control Zones (Consolidation of Interventions)	Low transmission Pre-Elimination Zones (Slide positivity rate <5% among suspected cases)
IRS			
Universal IRS		√	√
Focalized IRS for epidemic response		√	√
ITNs			
ITN universal coverage	√	√	
ITN coverage in households at increased risk			√
Routine ITN distribution	√	√	
Focalized ITN distribution in response to epidemics		√	√
IPTp			
IPTp among pregnant women	√	√	
Case management			
Diagnostic case confirmation	√	√	√
ACTs for confirmed cases	√	√	
Radical treatment (ACT plus primaquine) for confirmed cases			√
Surveillance			
Weekly surveillance	√	√	√
Active case detection during an epidemic (ACTS for confirmed cases)	√	√	
Active case detection, around a case (ACT + PQ for confirmed cases)			√

The National Strategy includes the following criteria for each phase of malaria control based on WHO guidelines:

Control zone applies to areas where: parasitemia prevalence among children under 5 years old is ≥2%, microscopy and RDT test positivity rate >5%, at least 10% of the population is tested, and the annual number of malaria cases (Annual Parasite Incidence) is >10 cases/1000 population. There are two types of control phases:
   1) control phase 1: where the zone has less than 80% coverage of malaria interventions and the priority is on scaling up interventions

2) control consolidation phase: where the area has more than 80% coverage of malaria interventions and the priority is on maintaining high coverage and reinforcing surveillance to move to pre-elimination phase.

Pre-elimination zone applies to areas where: parasitemia prevalence among children under 5 years old is <2%, microscopy and RDT test positivity rate is <5%, at least 10% of the population is being tested, and the API is <10 cases/1000 population.

There are presently no pre-elimination zones in Madagascar; however, the NMCP is currently putting in place all measures necessary to declare certain districts as pre-elimination districts. While some limited geographic zones may meet some of the pre-elimination criteria (for example <5% test positivity rate and <10 cases/1000 population reported through health facilities), data are still inadequate to be able to confirm all criteria are met to classify a zone as pre-elimination and shift to a pre-elimination strategy. As such, the current focus is on control until the pre-elimination criteria are confirmed and remain stable over time.

ITNs: In 2008, a major strategic change regarding ITN distribution in Madagascar occurred, moving from targeted distribution of ITNs to vulnerable groups to universal coverage, defined in the 2008-2012 National Strategy as two nets per household. The goal of two nets per household is applicable to all 92 malaria endemic districts, but excluded the 19 health districts of the Central Highlands that receive IRS and where epidemic surveillance systems are in place. According to the 2008-2009 DHS, the average household size in Madagascar is 4.7 (4.8 in the rural areas). In order to achieve the objective of two ITNs per household, the distribution methodology of one ITN per three persons during free mass campaigns (which translates into one ITN per 2.4 persons) was adopted to ensure equity.

Madagascar prioritizes free ITN distribution through mass campaigns as the primary approach to scaling up to universal coverage. In addition, three "keep up" strategies are supported: routine distribution of free ITNs through antenatal care (ANC) and expanded program on immunization (EPI) clinics targeting pregnant women and infants; free targeted distribution to communities most affected by natural disasters, such as cyclones; and the sale of highly subsidized ITNs in some peri-urban communities.

Under the 2013–2017 National Strategic Plan, the universal coverage goal was changed from two ITNs per household to one ITN for every two persons. The ITN-targeted area was expanded to include one district that was previously targeted with IRS and where IPTp is a strategy, thus bringing the total target area to 93 out of 112 health districts. By the end of 2015, the goal is for at least 80% of all households in targeted districts to own at least one ITN per two persons.

IRS: The 2013-2017 National Strategic Plan calls for focalized IRS stratified by commune in three geographic zones, which have completed three to four consecutive years of blanket IRS: the Central Highlands (CHL); the Fringe areas bordering the CHL; and districts to the west and south of the Fringe. Blanket IRS was coupled with free mass ITN distribution in 37 out of the 53 districts that received since 2010–2011. These included all IRS districts except for those in the CHL. At the end of the 2011 spray round, the CHL and Fringe districts (32 districts) completed four consecutive years of universal IRS coverage and transitioned to spraying in the 30% of communes with the highest malaria transmission, based on the incidence of reported malaria at health facilities. By the end of the 2012 spray round, the extension districts to the South and West (21 districts) had received three consecutive years of blanket IRS coverage and all 53 districts will be transitioning to focalized IRS. Focalized IRS includes only the highest transmission communes for spraying and relies on malaria surveillance and response planning to prevent epidemics. Approximately 30% of all communes will undergo spraying prioritized based on clinical and entomological data that show the highest levels of ongoing transmission.

IPTp: IPTp has been implemented since 2004 in 93 fringe and coastal districts where malaria transmission is stable or seasonal. The policy excludes the 19 districts in the CHL, which are epidemic prone. The malaria in pregnancy (MIP) strategy includes the provision and promotion of ITN use during pregnancy and IPTp, delivered as a package during ANC visits. The IPTp policy calls for two doses of sulfadoxine-pyrimethamine (SP) to be taken at least one month apart: the first dose after quickening and the second dose one month later.

In 2013, the National Malaria Control Program will meet to discuss WHO's new IPTp guidelines and discuss updating the strategy as a result. By 2015, Madagascar aims to have 75% of pregnant women in the covered districts receiving two doses of IPTp, and 85% receiving at least one dose. Administration of IPTp should be directly observed and free-of-charge. CHWs play an essential role in promoting the use of antenatal services. All focused antenatal care (FANC), including tetanus vaccination and malaria prevention activities, is integrated at the CSB level. The NMCP works closely with the *Direction de la Santé de l'Enfant, de la Mère et de la Reproduction* (Directorate of Child and Maternal Health and Reproductive Health) to plan and implement MIP activities, including IPTp. The NMCP has also included IPTp as part of integrated ANC services package during the mother and child health promotion weeks held twice a year in April and October. In addition to ANC counseling activities, these biannual health weeks distribute vitamin A and deworming medicines to children 6 – 59 months, and iron, and folic acid to pregnant women, conduct mass immunization campaigns, and disseminate health promotion messages.

Case Management: ACTs were adopted as the first-line treatment for malaria in 2005. ACTs and RDTs were rolled out in public health facilities from late 2006 through 2008 and at the community level in late 2008. The NMCP policy requires that, where possible, all cases of malaria be diagnosed by microscopy or RDT, including at the community level. Where biological diagnosis is not possible, diagnosis should be based on clinical evaluation and treatment should be provided after other causes of fever have been excluded.

The 2013–2017 National Strategic Plan calls for correct and timely diagnosis and treatment of at least 95% of malaria cases seen at health facilities. In pre-elimination districts, the national strategy calls for use of RDTs coupled with progressive use of microscopy and eventual use of molecular testing from filter paper blood spots. The plan sets a target for correct case management, including biological diagnosis using microscopy or RDTs, of at least 80% of fever cases among children under five years old evaluated and treatment at the community level within 24 hours of fever onset. First-line treatment is artesunate-amodiaquine (AS/AQ) (except for pregnant women in their first trimester, in which case treatment is oral quinine); in pre-elimination zones, the national strategy also calls for administration of a single dose of Primaquine in addition to AS/AQ for cases of simple malaria, except in pregnant women and children less than four years of age. Treatment of severe malaria is injectable artesunate at the hospital level. Rectal artesunate should be administered as a pre-referral treatment at community and health facility level for symptoms of severe malaria in children less than five years. As of mid-2013, injectable artesunate and pre-referral rectal artesunate have not yet rolled out but this is planned to occur in 2014.

PMI has supported the training of more than 8,500 CHWs in integrated community case management in rural communities located at more than five kilometers from the nearest health facility, covering about one-third of those communities nationwide. The Global Fund is also supporting the scale up of CHWs, and with support from these donors, by the end of 2012, over 35,000 CHWs were trained in over 17,500 fokontanies. CHWs have been trained to use RDTs to confirm all malaria cases. They are also trained in integrated case management of diarrhea and pneumonia, providing treatment with oral rehydration salts plus zinc and cotrimoxazole, respectively.

The national strategy objectives for the management of malaria commodities are as follows:
In areas in the malaria control/consolidation phase:
- At least 95% of health facilities experience no stock-out of RDTs and ACTs of longer than one week over the previous three months
- At least 95% of health facilities experience no stock-outs of SP or ITNs of longer than one week over the previous three months

In areas in the malaria pre-elimination phase:
- 100% of districts have a system of routine quality assurance and quality control
- No clinic experiences a stock-out of RDTs or ACTs of more than one week over the previous three months

5. Integration, Collaboration, and Coordination

Several donors and partners support malaria interventions in Madagascar, including PMI, the Global Fund, UNICEF, WHO, the Principality of Monaco, *Institut Pasteur de Madagascar* (IPM) and Roll Back Malaria (RBM)/Southern Africa Regional Network, with the NMCP coordinating all partners. Under NMCP leadership, a strong local RBM partnership has been established, and committee meetings are held monthly. RBM partners worked closely to oversee and conduct the MIS 2011, to plan and design the Malaria Program Review (July 2011), to organize and facilitate a national conference on pre-elimination (November 2011), to inform the new 2013–2017 National Strategic Plan, to conduct the November/December 2012 mass distribution of over 3.5 million ITNs in 31 East Coast districts, and to coordinate technical assistance as needed at all levels. Currently, RBM partners are implementing the 2013 MIS, and preparing the August/September 2013 mass distribution of over 6 million nets to cover 62 additional districts, thus covering all the 93 districts targeted for ITNs in a window of 10 months.

With FY 2014 funding PMI will continue to seek opportunities to collaborate with USG health programs to ensure maximum impact for every health dollar the USG invests in the country. The integration of maternal and child health services and malaria is an example of support.. Since malaria prevention and control activities have been implemented as part of integrated maternal and child health services, PMI will contribute to strengthening capacity to deliver these services. PMI will work with other USG-funded programs and other partners to support the comprehensive primary health care package, including the training and implementation of community-based diagnosis and treatment of fever, IPTp, and early correct case management. With FY 2014 resources, PMI will continue to support universal coverage of ITNs via mass distribution campaign and various keep-up distribution methods.

6. Goal and Targets of the President's Malaria Initiative

The goal of PMI is to reduce malaria-associated mortality by 70% compared to pre-Initiative levels in the 15 original PMI countries. By the end of 2014, PMI will assist Madagascar to move towards achieving the following targets in populations at risk for malaria:

- >90% of households with a pregnant woman and/or children under five will own at least one ITN;
- 85% of children under five will have slept under an ITN the previous night;
- 85% of pregnant women will have slept under an ITN the previous night;
- 85% of houses in geographic areas targeted for IRS will have been sprayed;
- 85% of pregnant women and children under five will have slept under an ITN the previous night or in a house that has been sprayed with IRS in the last 12 months;
- 85% of women who have completed a pregnancy in the last two years will have received two or more doses of IPTp during that pregnancy; and
- 85% of children under five with suspected malaria will have received treatment with ACTs within 24 hours of onset of their symptoms.
- 85% of government health facilities will have ACTs available for the treatment of uncomplicated malaria

Because PMI does not directly support the Government of Madagascar (GoM), there will be no PMI-attributable impact on the last target listed above.

7. Current Status of Malaria Indicators

The most recent DHS was carried out from November 2008 to August 2009 and provides baseline indicators for PMI in Madagascar. Child mortality was estimated at 72 per 1,000 live births by the direct method. Additional data, including routine malaria-specific HMIS data and malaria program data compiled by the NMCP, are reported and centrally stored in a national malaria database. Some national malaria indicators have been estimated based on these data and additional sources such as special studies and limited surveys. The 2013 MIS is underway and preliminary results are expected in September 2013. Results for these malaria indicators are summarized in the tables below.

Health facility utilization is low and chloroquine and SP are still widely available on the market for self-treatment and prescription by private providers. Furthermore, many providers treat uncomplicated malaria with intramuscular injections of quinine, which are not free of charge (ACTWatch Surveys 2010, 2011).

Table 2: Nationwide household survey results, Madagascar 2008-2011

Indicator	2008-2009 DHS (PMI baseline)	2011 MIS
Proportion of all households with at least one ITN	73%	94%
Average number of ITNs per household[1]	1.1	1.8
Proportion of households with at least one ITN for every two people [1]	23%	37%
Proportion of population with access to an ITN within their household [1]	44%	67%
Proportion of individuals who slept under an ITN the previous night [1]	48%	82%
Proportion of children under five years old who slept under an ITN the previous night[1]	58%	89%
Proportion of pregnant women who slept under an ITN the previous night[1]	58%	85%
Proportion of women who received two or more doses of IPTp during their last pregnancy in the last two years[2]	8%	22%
Proportion of houses sprayed with IRS in the 12 months preceding the survey[3]	Not available	79%
Proportion of population who slept under an ITN the previous night or in a house that has been sprayed with IRS in the last 12 months	Not available[4]	87%
Proportion of children under five years old with fever in the last two weeks who had a finger or heel stick	Not available	6%
Proportion of children under five years old with fever in the last two weeks for whom advice or treatment was sought from a health facility or provider	41%	34%
Proportion receiving ACTs, among children under five years old with fever in the last two weeks who received any antimalarial drugs	5%	19%
Proportion Receiving First-Line Treatment According to National Policy Among Children Under Five Years Old with Fever in the Last Two Weeks Who Received Any Antimalarial Drugs	2%	15%
Proportion of children under 5 years old with fever in the last 2 weeks who received treatment with ACTs within 24 hours of onset of fever	0.4%	3%

Proportion of government health facilities that have ACTs available for treatment of uncomplicated malaria	Not available	Not available

[1]Among 92 targeted districts receive LLINs per the national strategy 2008-2012
[2]Among 93 districts targeted districts benefit from IPTp
[3]Among 53 targeted health districts that benefit from IRS per the national strategy 2008-2012
[4]The DHS 2008/2099 did not collect information on IRS

Table 3: Impact indicators

Indicator	2008/2009 DHS (PMI baseline)	MIS 2011
All-cause under five mortality rate (Direct method)	72/1000 live births	Not available
All-cause under five mortality rate (Indirect, Brass method)	83/1000 live births	91/1000 live births
Proportion of children aged 6-59 months with malaria parasitemia	Not available	6.2%
Proportion of children aged 6-59 months with a hemoglobin of <8 g/dL	2.5%	1.4%

8. Challenges, Opportunities, and Threats

Due to the political constraints related to working with the Government of Madagascar (GoM) since March 2009, the USG and some other donors have not been able to support health interventions, such as malaria case management or capacity building in the public health sector. Inadequate supervision, lack of refresher training, staffing shortages, incomplete and inaccurate reporting, and commodity stock-outs have continued to pose challenges across the public health services and the NMCP. The NMCP along with partners has employed CHWs to deliver iCCM for malaria, pneumonia, and diarrhea. However, results from a CHW assessment conducted in 2011 showed weaknesses in the ability of CHWs to assess symptoms, determine the correct diagnosis, and administer a correct treatment or refer. Only 51% of the CHWs observed performed satisfactorily compared to a gold standard measurement.

Parallel supply chain systems exist in Madagascar: one for the public sector and one for socially marketed products. Highly subsidized sales of health commodities through social marketing have been promoted historically in Madagascar with funding both from the Global Fund as well as the USG. However, weak commodity management, delays due to late financing, and inadequate stock management and information systems lead to stock-outs. PMI and Global Fund are coordinating efforts to improve supply chain management for the social marketing products; the EU and the French Cooperation are supporting the strengthening of SALAMA.

An estimated 50–60% of the population does not seek care in health facilities when they are ill; some rely on self-treatment with drugs purchased from the informal sector. An assessment of the national pharmaceutical management capacity in 2008 highlighted several constraints: (1) lack of trained pharmacists in public pharmacies; (2) weak institutional capacity; (3) insufficient pharmaceutical policies and guidelines; (4) low capacity and inadequate human resources for pharmaceutical management in the health care system; (5) multiple vertical health programs lacking integration and coordination; and (6) logistics and distribution challenges at the peripheral level. These constraints still remain. The adoption and expansion of the community health services through the established CHWs to conduct preventive activities and iCCM is a partial but significant response to improving access to services and care seeking behaviors.

9. PMI Support Strategy and Expected Results

Within a year after release of FY 2014 funding:

Prevention:
1. PMI will have supported targeted IRS in 15 districts, covering approximately 396,000 structures.
2. PMI will have procured approximately 2.8 million ITNs for the 2015 universal coverage campaign in Madagascar.

Case management:
1. Home-based management of malaria will continue to reach over 50% of all communes located more than five kilometers from a health facility in the twelve regions supported by USAID nationwide, providing diagnosis with RDTs and treatment with an ACT to more than 35% of children under five years old with fever. This will be done as part of iCCM which will also provide treatment as needed for acute respiratory infections and diarrhea.

2. PMI will have procured approximately 2.25 million RDTs for trained CHWs and FBOs/NGOs. The Global Fund plans to fill the entire ACT gap, therefore PMI is not planning to procure ACTs at this time.

3. PMI will have procured approximately 3 million tablets of iron and folic acid for distribution via CHWs to pregnant women.

III. OPERATIONAL PLAN

1. Insecticide-Treated Nets

NMCP and PMI Objectives
Under the 2013-2017 National Strategic Plan, Madagascar has adopted one ITN for every two persons to achieve universal coverage for all zones in the control and consolidation phase, and coverage of households at increased risks and in epidemic response in the pre-elimination phase. There are presently no pre-elimination zones in Madagascar; however, the NMCP is currently putting in place all measures necessary to declare certain districts "pre-elimination districts.

Progress since PMI was launched
Madagascar completed nationwide, mass campaigns to delivery free ITNs to reach all persons living in malaria endemic areas in 2009-2010 and again in 2012-2013. The 2009-2010 campaign achieved an average of 1.8 ITNs per household compared to the then national target of two ITNs per household. This resulted in high ownership with 94% of households reporting ownership of at least one ITN six months after the campaign compared to 72% in 2008-2009.[8] These results were similar by geographic zone, household economic status, and households with and without children under five. Furthermore, 82% of all individuals sleeping in the household the night before the survey reported sleeping under an ITN and there was even higher usage among children under five and pregnant women (89% and 85% respectively).

The 2012 and 2013 mass campaigns were conducted following the earlier strategy of two ITNs per household (equating to about 1 ITN: 2.4 persons) and delivered ITNs to 31 districts on the East Coast in 2012 and the remaining 62 endemic districts by the end of 2013.

Several reports, including a limited PMI-supported assessment of net durability that looked at ITNs three years after delivery, indicate a rapid decline in net survivorship in Madagascar. This highlights the need to support delivery of ITNs between campaigns to maintain high coverage. Two channels have been traditionally used in Madagascar to delivery ITNs between campaigns: delivery through routine ANC and expanded program on immunizations (EPI) clinics and social marketing. Both were limited by net availability and far too few nets have been delivered to effectively or equitably cover the anticipated yearly ITN losses across the general population. PMI/Madagascar is testing two other channels to improve availability and distribution of ITNs free-of-charge on a more continuous basis. These channels are community-based interventions using CHWs to delivery ITNs to pregnant women and to households on an as-needed basis. PMI also distributes ITNs to communities in response to epidemics or disasters, such as cyclones. The channels supported by PMI in Madagascar are listed in Table 4.

---

[8] DHS 2008/9

Table 4: Madagascar's national ITN distribution strategies for ITN targeted districts in control or consolidation phase

Type of ITN Distribution	Strategy	Approach	Target Pop	Geographic Areas
Free Distribution	Catch-Up	Mass Campaign	One ITN per 2 persons in 93 of the 112 health districts	93 out of the 112 health districts
	Keep-Up	Delivery to pregnant women at community level by CHWs (pending pilot results)	Pregnant women	As many of the 93 endemic districts as feasible
	Keep-Up	Community-based distribution through CHWs to those needing LLINs (pending pilot results)	General population based on a pull model driven by those who need nets seeking nets through a CHW system	93 out of the 112 health districts;
	Emergency Response	Distribution in response to natural disasters and emergencies	One ITN per two persons in communities most affected by natural disasters, such as cyclones	Communities most affected by natural disasters such as cyclones
Social marketing	Keep-Up	Social marketing; commercial sales of subsidized nets	Those who can afford subsidized nets	Targeted peri-urban areas among the LLIN targeted health districts

Progress during the past 12 months
With FY 2011 funds, PMI procured 2.1 million ITNs and provided logistics and operational costs for their delivery to inhabitants in 19 districts on the East Coast, a region that last received ITNs in 2009, during the initial phase of the first national mass campaign. The second round of national mass campaigns began November/December 2012 and followed the existing national policy of two ITNs per household, or the equivalent of 1 ITN per 2.4 persons. An additional 12 districts on the East Coast were included in phase one and received 1.44 million Global Fund-procured ITNs in December 2012/January 2013. PMI has also promoted BCC activities and campaign planning support through bilateral projects in 19 districts and through an extensive network of Peace Corps volunteers in Madagascar.

With FY 2012 funds, PMI procured 2.2 million ITNs to support a mass campaign in 2013 to cover 28 of the remaining 62 districts that last received ITNs in 2010. Global Fund has procured 3.5 million ITNs to cover 33 districts for this second phase of the national campaign. The campaign will be rolled out as shown in Figure 3 below.

Figure 3: Distribution of districts targeted for rolling ITN distribution campaign, by year

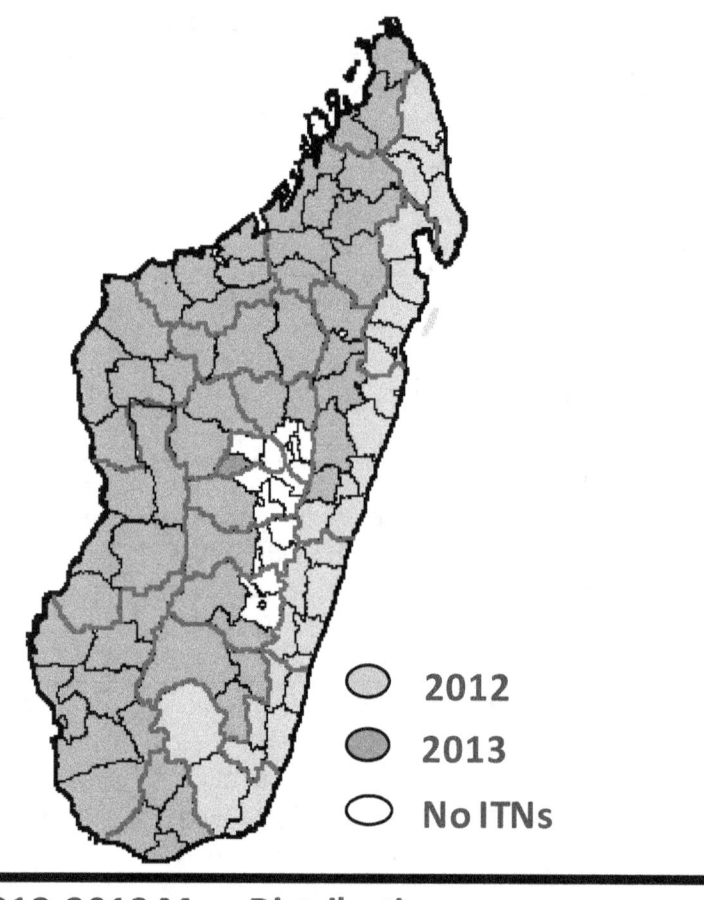

2012
2013
No ITNs

2012-2013 Mass Distribution Replacement Campaign

With FY 2012 funds, PMI is supporting a pilot in one district of a community-based approach to deliver ITNs on an as-needed basis. With FY 2013 funds, it is supporting the scale up of this approach to 31 additional districts on the East Coast that received ITNs during the 2012 universal campaign. The approach relies on CHWs and local leaders to manage the distribution of ITNs to inhabitants meeting criteria for an ITN replacement.

If results from the pilot are positive, with FY 2013 funds PMI will support developing a community-based channel for delivery of ITNs to pregnant women that will be launched in as many of the 93 malaria endemic districts as feasible in the first year. In addition to delivering ITNs, CHWs will encourage pregnant women to frequently attend ANC clinics and inform them about the benefits of IPTp. The effectiveness will be evaluated to ensure high, equitable coverage in ITNs can be maintained between mass campaigns.

To complement these free distribution channels, PMI has supported social marketing of highly subsidized ITNs, at a price of approximately $1.50 per net to the end user. The social marketing approach is focused on peri-urban areas on the East Coast.

Table 5: Source and method of distribution of LLINs for 2012 and projected for 2013 through 2015

Method	Source	2012	2013[1]	2014[2]	2015[3]	Total 2012-2015
Mass Distribution	PMI	2,100,000	2,700,000	0	2,800,000	7,600,000
	Global Fund	1,442,314	3,515,320	210,000	0	5,167,634
Routine ANC/EPI	PMI	0	0	0	0	0
	Global Fund	128,000	492,000	0	475,000	1,095,000
CHWs to pregnant women	PMI	0	0	750,000	0	750,000
	Global Fund	0	0	0	0	0
CHWs to Households	PMI	0	15,000	340,000	325000	680,000
	Global Fund	0	0	0	0	0
Emergencies and Disaster Response	PMI	0	0	50,000	0	50,000
	Global Fund	44,000	10,500	200,000	200,000	454,500
Social marketing[4]	PMI	0	0	200,000	0	200,000
	Global Fund	21,341	399,000	0	0	420,341
Total		**3,735,655**	**7,131,820**	**1,750,000**	**3,800,000**	**16,417,475**

Notes:

[1] Reflects expected total distribution achieved by December 31, 2013, based on current estimates /plans

[2] Reflects expected total distribution achieved by December 31, 2014, based on current estimates/ plans.

[3] Reflects expected total distribution achieved by December 31, 2015, based on current estimates/ plans.

[4] Reflects the number distributed to retail outlets or distribution warehouses from the central level

PMI conducted an assessment of the physical durability of nets distributed in late 2009. Among 500 polyester and polyethylene ITNs tagged and examined 3 years later, only 152 (30%) remained in the households. Of those nets no longer present it is not known what proportion were lost due to attrition unrelated to physical durability (e.g. given away) and what proportion were no longer present due to loss of physical integrity. Among the 152 remaining nets found in households at 3 years, 80% were considered "serviceable."[9] Beginning in 2013, PMI will monitor the physical durability of ITNs distributed as part of the mass campaigns in 62 districts in 2013.

Plans and Justification
Mass campaign in 2015 to replace ITNs distributed to 31 districts the East Coast in 2012:

FY 2014 funds will be used to support phase one of Madagascar's third national scale mass campaign beginning in 2015. This will cover approximately 7.043 million inhabitants in 31 districts on the East Coast who received ITNs in the 2012 mass campaign. Phase two, in 2016, will reach approximately 10.2 million inhabitants living in the 62 districts that received ITNs in 2013. PMI will support continuous distribution of ITNs to the 31 East Coast districts in 2013 and 2014 and, depending on the success of those efforts, it may be possible to reduce the quantity needed for the universal coverage mass campaign in 2015.

PMI will only have sufficient funds to procure a proportion of the ITNs needed to cover the 31 East Coast districts. Additional ITNs will be needed from other donors to fill the gap for the campaign, to cover the needs for continuous distribution and to provide nets in response to emergencies. PMI will focus on the East Coast which has the highest malaria prevalence in the country, perennial transmission, and is not covered by IRS.

PMI has experienced recent malaria epidemics in the south of the country and PMI will remain ready to provide support, as appropriate under the current suspension, for malaria treatment and prevention in the affected to area. PMI will continue to monitor the durability of ITNs on a small scale that will look only at physical durability. This activity will also assess the main causes for loss of ITN physical integrity with the goal of working to improve household care of ITNs.

Challenges, opportunities, threats
Malaria transmission in Madagascar has been decreasing over the last decade with the scale-up of prevention and case management activities. In the first half of 2012 an epidemic of malaria occurred in a historically endemic zone of Madagascar. The epidemic had 2.5–10 times the number of malaria cases seen in recent years and affected all age groups. An investigation showed that net ownership and use declined substantially in the affected zone only 2.5 years after the last free mass distribution campaign. An increased risk of malaria infection may have resulted from decreased malaria immunity in the population and loss of protection provided by viable ITNs. These findings underscore the need for maintaining high malaria prevention coverage and improving surveillance and epidemic preparedness. The survivorship and physical integrity of ITNs in Madagascar are currently being monitored to help inform ITN keep-up and replacement needs between campaigns.

Delays in procurement and delivery of ITNs from other donors have been a major challenge for the timing and effectiveness of mass campaigns in Madagascar. Until now, routine distribution through health facilities has been hampered by a lack of ITNs as a result of prioritizing large

---

[9] Guidelines for monitoring the durability of long-lasting insecticidal mosquito nets under operational conditions. WHO, 2011. http://whqlibdoc.who.int/publications/2011/9789241501705_eng.pdf

mass campaigns (given equitable coverage results) and logistics challenges of maintaining adequate stocks of nets in remote health facilities.

The capacity to effectively deliver relatively large quantities of ITNs through community-based approaches has not yet been assessed and there may be significant logistical challenges to rapid scale up both for community-based delivery to pregnant women and to households needing an ITN.

Anecdotal reports indicate that misuse of ITNs for fishing may be a serious issue in some riverine areas. Misuse is also known to occur in other settings as well, to protect crops or even livestock. PMI will work with local authorities, focusing first on riverine areas where use of net for fishing might be a problem, to encourage strong action against misuse of ITNs and provide authorities with examples of what has worked in other sites to mitigate this problem. Qualitative data collected during recent studies and supervision visits point to potential reasons for sub-optimal use of ITNs among a relatively small proportion of the population. Some families "hoard" nets and continue to use their old net in order to ensure they have enough nets over time; other families have small houses which makes it difficult to suspend more than one net at a time, even if they have large families. There is currently no information regarding how big a problem these factors are. PMI will work with local partners to find ways to promote appropriate ITN use in an on-going fashion.

Gap Analysis

Table 6: Gap analysis

Calendar Year	2014[1]	2015[1]
Population of 93 targeted ITN districts	**16,705,932**	**17,207,110**
Continuous Distribution ANC/EPI Distribution Needs		
Pregnant women attending health facilities (2.3% of the population); 80% attendance at ANC clinics	307,389	180,468[2]
Children < 1 year old (3.9% of the population); 90% EPI attendance	586,378	344,263[2]
Estimated total need for routine services	*893,767*	*524,731*
Continuous Distribution – Community-Based to Replace Worn Out Nets[3]		
For 31 districts East Coast – universal coverage campaign in 2012	820,000	0
For 62 districts – universal coverage campaign in 2013	552,000	828,000[2]
Estimated total for replacement of expired ITNs	*1,372,000*	*828,000*
Total Routine and Replacement ITN Needs	**2,265,767**	**1,352,731**
Inputs to Continuous Distribution		
ITNs available for continuous distribution	1,400,000	0
ITNs available for emergencies	250,000	200,000
Social marketing ITNs	200,000	0
Total ITN inputs	**1,850,000**	**200,000**
Continuous Distribution Net Gap	**415,767**	**1,152,731**
Universal Coverage Campaign Needs[4]		
Population of 31 targeted ITN districts	7,297,965	7,485,093
Total Mass Campaign Need (based on 1:1.8 ratio)	0[5]	4,158,385
Total donor ITN input for a 2015 campaign	**0[5]**	**3,174.350**
East Coast Mass Campaign Net Gap		**984,385**

1. PMI and Global Fund are the sources of ITNs for these interventions.
2. Continuous needs for 62 districts (57% of the population) not covered by the mass campaign.
3. Net loss calculated using the generally accepted ITN loss rate of 8% in the first 12 months and 20% after 24 months.
4. Only those areas needing campaign in 2014 or 2015 considered; 62 malaria endemic districts not included for this reason
5. Universal campaign within the past three years; no ITNs for campaigns needed.

Proposed activities with FY 2014 funding ($13,473,950)

Based on these assumptions and identified needs, the specific activities supported by PMI in FY 2014 include:

1. *Procure LLINs for mass distribution:* To procure about 2.8 million LLINs for distribution to 31 districts on the East Coast that last received LLINs through a mass campaign in late 2012. Assumes a cost of $3.60/LLIN with delivery from port to central warehouse. *($10,249,950)*

2. *Technical assistance for procurement and supply chain management* for all malaria commodities. PMI's implementing partner supports a small team who works with in country partners on improving commodity management. With regards to LLINs, the team works to coordinate the procurement, shipping, customs clearance, warehousing, and transportation of nets. The $300K cover staff, office and warehouse renting, operational and utility costs *($300,000)*

3. *Distribution of ITNs for 2015 campaign on the East Coast*: targeting 31 districts that received LLIN through a mass campaign in late 2012 and have been targeted for continuous distribution in 2013 and 2014. *($2,800,000)*

4. *Support for continued assessment of net durability*: Includes monitoring the physical durability of different brands of LLINs that will be distributed as part of mass campaigns in 2013. This supports the second-year data collection. *($50,000)*

5. *Support Malaria Peace Corps Volunteer (PCV):* Provide support for a PCV to promote malaria prevention and correct use and care of ITNs and monitor ITN distribution activities. PCV will be nested with an implementing partner and funds include the cost of housing, transportation and equipment. *($12,000)*

6. *Technical assistance to LLIN activities:* PMI will provide one CDC staff TDY to provide TA for monitoring and evaluation of LLIN activities. *($12,000)*

7. *Epidemic response:* Distribution of LLINs in response to emergencies and/or epidemics *($50,000)*

2. Indoor Residual Spraying

NMCP/PMI Objectives

The National Malaria Control Strategic Plan[10] calls for the use of insecticide-based vector control measures, including IRS, to prevent transmission of *P. falciparum* malaria. IRS in 2012-2013 targeted the central highlands and near-by margin districts, as well as the 'epidemic' southern region and the West Coast (Figure 4).

---

[10] Plan Stratégique de Lutte contre le Paludisme à Madagascar, PNLP, 2013-2017

Figure 4: IRS (2012-2013) areas: PMI (light blue-dark blue), GFAMT (tan-brown)

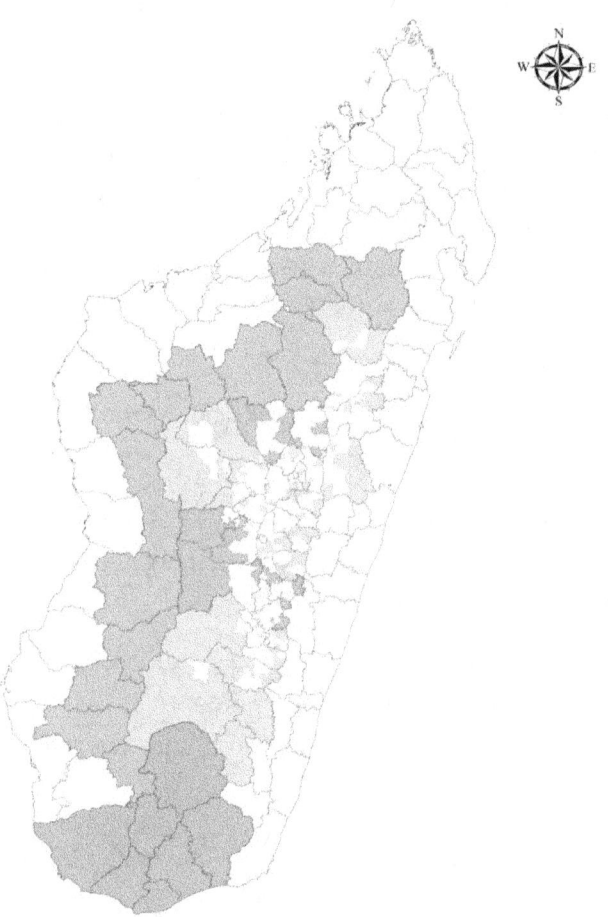

In application of the National Strategic Plan, universal coverage (district-wide spraying) in the highlands was replaced by focalized spraying, where IRS is done only in selected communes (sub-districts). The decision to spray a commune is based on the relative intensity of transmission, estimated from clinical case data. Communes are ranked (stratified), using this criteria, and the top 30% are selected for IRS. Stratification, while attractive in theory, may be problematic because of the variable quality and completeness of health facility data used to stratify sub-districts. A PMI operations research proposal to evaluate the validity of health center clinical data for stratification, funded with FY 2012 and 2013 funds, is planned.

Moving the PMI IRS activity to locations where transmission is more uniform (thereby avoiding the issue of stratification), is not a realistic option. The ITN and IRS strategies (target areas), described in the National Strategy are supported by different partners and carefully integrated to maximize coverage. Given the level of coordination, it is unlikely that an 'independent' shift of IRS would improve things. PMI IRS target districts are now in the fringe zones between CHL and coastal areas, as well as the epidemic zones in the South. The fringe sites have a more seasonal transmission pattern. Therefore spraying is more likely to contribute to reduced morbidity and mortality. Moving IRS to areas of even higher transmission, i.e., the coastal region, is not in line with PMI guidance due to the length of the transmission season and the duration of insecticide residual effect.

Due to the threat of epidemic malaria in the South, IRS activity is also informed by a surveillance system for early detection of malaria outbreaks. However, there is no mechanism for IRS rapid response, once an epidemic is declared. National surveillance and response guidelines are being revised (in 2013) and will include a more detailed response plan with criteria for inclusion of IRS as part of the response effort.

Progress during the last 12 months
From October to December 2012, PMI supported the annual IRS campaign in seven highland-margin districts. Approximately 87,000 structures were sprayed, protecting a population of around 500,000. PMI also supported IRS in eight districts in the South, between February and April 2013, Approximately 284,103 structures were sprayed, protecting a population of around 1,258,539; however, access to some areas was disrupted due to political unrest.

In response to the challenge of insecticide resistance, a monitoring activity, supported in part by PMI, continued to identify and map resistant vector populaions across the country. The results inform insecticide procurement decisions, in accordance with WHO IRS insecticide rotation strategy.[11] For example, resistance to the carbamate-class insecticides, used for IRS from 2008-2012, and documented, with increasing frequency, since 2011,[12] was seen again in 2013. Resistant vector poulations included both *An. funestus* (one population in the Central Highlands) and *An. gambaie s.l.* (four populations, from both the Highlands and the West). As a result, the carbamate-class IRS product will be replaced by an organophosphate (OP) class product in 2013-2014. The situation *vis à vis* pyrethroid resistance is more problematic. Resistance surveillance in 2013 detected eleven *An. gambaie s.l.* pyrethorid - resistant populations, located in IRS and ITN areas of the country.

Plans and Justification
PMI will support IRS with an OP insecticide in approximately 30 percent of the communes in its assigned IRS districts (Central Highlands, margin areas, South). Use of a capsule suspension (*cs*)-formulation OP insecticide for longer effectiveness is recommended, especially in the South, where one, well-timed, annual spray round could provide protection throughout the seasonal 'epidemic' period. The final number of structures to be sprayed in the South, estimated to be around 300,000, will be determined by the cost of the insecticide, which, unfortunately, is twice that of the carbamate insecticide used in 2013.

PMI will continue to support vector-insecticide resistance monitoring at ten sites in 2014. These will be located in IRS and ITN areas in order to monitor the spread of resistance and to inform an IRS insecticide rotation plan, designed to stay ahead of the looming threat of an operational IRS failure assoicated with vector resistance. In ITN sites where pyrethroid resistance levels are increasing, assessment of the physiological mechanism(s) responsible for resistance will be

---

[11] Global Plan for Insecticide Resistance Management (GPIRM), WHO 2012
[12] PMI Malaria Operations Plan 2013, Table 7, Insecticide resistance in Madagascar 2010-2011

carried out to better inform net procurement.[13] Monitoring will focus on three objectives: (1) mapping the distribution and intensity of resistance, (2) evaluation of the physiological mechanism responsible for pyrethroid resistance, and (3) assessing the impact of insecticide rotation on occurrence and intensity of vector resistance.

Challenges, Opportunities and Threats
Challenge: *IRS coordination.* Madagascar has been under U.S. Department of State restrictions that limit PMI involvement with the NMCP. At the same time, the country faces a number of challenges to the IRS strategy that require coordinated action by all partners. This is especially true for: responding to epidemic malaria, vector-insecticide resistance management, and IRS insecticide rotation.

Opportunities: *Encourage donors to provide ongoing support to IRS.* Madagascar has a strong national malaria control program. Unfortunately resources to continue IRS may decline prior to the 2015 spray round, when current Global Fund support ends (even with Global Fund and PMI assistance, IRS needs are not entirely covered). In such unpredictable times, PMI should continue to support this IRS program, and, more importantly, to promote confidence in the IRS approach through operations research on stratification, evaluation of new approaches and technologies for managing insecticide resistance, and assistance with identification of partners with resources for program costs.

Threats: *Resistance.* There is mounting evidence that insecticide (pyrethroid and carbamate) resistance is spreading. Each year, since its inception, the PMI-supported IRS entomology monitoring and evaluation activity has documented more cases of reduced insecticide susceptibility in areas where IRS and ITNs or a combination of both serve as primary deterrents to malaria transmission. Insecticide rotation (informed by comprehensive insecticide resistance surveillance) and introduction of new products that kill resistant vectors, are the best approaches at present. Longer-term solutions will be based on strategic planning and use of new products, e.g. insecticides with novel mechanisms not previously seen by vector populations.

Proposed activities with FY 2014 funding ($5,460,000)

1. *Support for IRS operations:* PMI will conduct focalized IRS operations, based on stratification and entomology monitoring and evaluation results in districts where PMI has supported spraying in the past. This includes support for: procurement of OP insecticides (ideally the long lasting *cs* formulation, which is currently awaiting WHO/WHOPES appproval) and IRS equipment, as well as training, safety- and environment-related protection, and appropriate supervision of all operational IRS activities. ($5,131,000)

2. *Support for IRS entomological monitoring:* PMI will support entomological monitoring and IRS impact assessment at ten location: two sites in each of the three IRS zones (highlands, margin distircts, South) and at four sites in non-IRS comparison areas. There will be new emphasis on evaluation of the physiological basis of vecor-pyrethroid resistance (as described in

---

[13] Permanet3.0® and Olyset Plus® LLINs developed to manage pyrethroid resistance associated with oxidase-based resistance mechanisms as well as providing protection to users. If oxidase mechanisms are responsible for pyrethroid resistance then investment in the new LLIN products may be justified.

PMI guidelines) to determine if new ITN products are an appropriate investment in Madagascar. Cost per site is estimated tobe $22,500, covering equipment, supplies, training, supervision, transportation and per diems. ($225,000)

3. *Support for entomological investigations during malaria epidemics*: PMI will continue to support *ad hoc* entomological assessments in response to epidemic alerts, with emphasis on investigations to incriminate the vector (taxonomy and density) and to assess its insecticide resistance profile and biting behaviour. ($80,000)

4. *Support for two IRS entomology IRS technical assistance visits*: CDC will carry out one trip to transfer technology to the implementing partner for assessment of the role of an oxidase-based mechanism in pyrethroid resistance and one trip to evaluate focal IRS using entomological measures of transmission. ($24,000)

3. Malaria in Pregnancy (MIP)

NMCP/PMI Objectives
As part of the national strategy to prevent and limit morbidity associated with malaria during pregnancy, IPTp has been implemented since 2004 in 92 (93 as of FY 2013) lowland and coastal districts where malaria transmission is stable or seasonal. The policy excludes the remaining 19 districts in the Central Highlands, which are epidemic prone. The strategy includes the provision and promotion of ITN use during pregnancy and early, frequent ANC visits to increase chances of completing IPTp, which is delivered as a package at ANC clinics. The IPTp policy calls for two doses of sulfadoxine-pyrimethamine (SP) taken at least one month apart: the first dose after quickening, and the second dose at least one month later. Administration of IPTp should be directly observed and free-of-charge.

Starting in 2004, the MoH trained health workers at CSBs on the provision of IPTp and plans to extend the training to the private sector with the support of Global Fund NSA funds. CHWs play an essential role in promoting the use of antenatal services, and is the cadre through which PMI supports all MIP activities; however, there are currently no plans to involve CHWs in the delivery of IPTp. All focused ANC, including tetanus vaccination and malaria prevention activities, are integrated at the level of the CSB. The NMCP works closely with the *Direction de la Santé de l'Enfant, de la Mère et de la Reproduction* (Directorate of Child and Maternal Health and Reproductive Health) to plan and implement MIP activities, including IPTp and ITN promotion. To further promote MIP interventions, the NMCP has included IPTp as part of integrated ANC services promoted during biannual outreach activities during the mother and child health promotion weeks in April and October. During these biannual health weeks, vitamin A and deworming medicines are distributed, mass immunization campaigns for children are conducted, ANC sensitization messages are provided to pregnant women, and health promotion messages are disseminated. Program surveillance data shows that IPTp uptake peaks during and right after the mother and child health weeks. In addition, the NMCP has initiated outreach activities consisting in going to villages for promotion of IPTp, identifying pregnant women and offering MIP package when feasible, and if funding is available.

The 2013–17 National Strategy objective calls for an increase in the uptake of the first dose and second dose of IPTp among pregnant women attending ANC clinics from 22 in 2011 to 80% in

2014 and 55% in 2011 to 70% 2014. The NMCP has revised the monthly HMIS reporting form to capture the number of women who receive both doses of SP for IPTp to monitor progress towards this goal.

Figure 5: Number of pregnant women benefiting from IPTp (2007-2011)

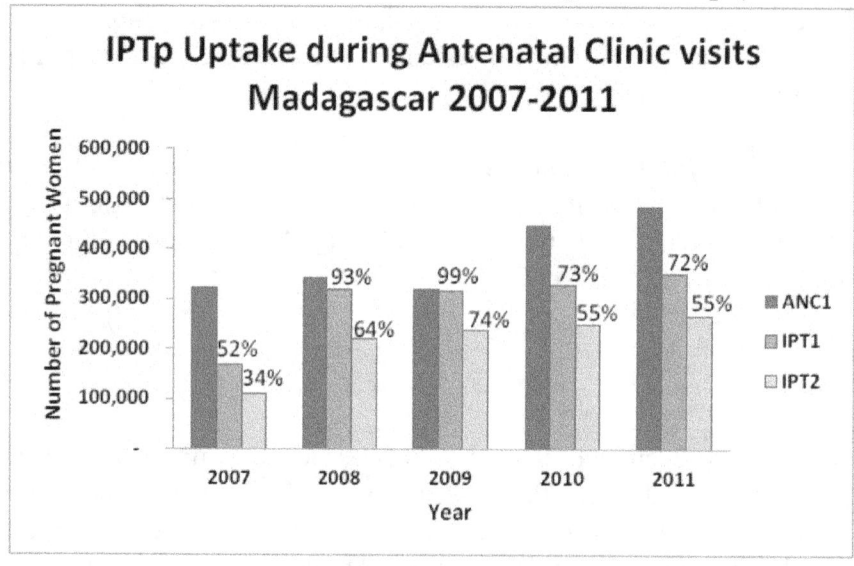

Source: HMIS and Global Malaria Program Country Profile (NMCP)

Progress during the last 12 months
In 2011, the HMIS reported that 73% of pregnant women attending ANC clinics at public health facilities took one dose of SP and 55% took two doses, a slight increase from previous years (Figure 5). All 2013 PMI-funded activities strengthening ANC/IPTp services delivered at public health facilities continues to be put on hold. PMI funding was used to support MIP activities by using CHWs to deliver BCC messages including the importance of seeking antenatal care, taking two doses of IPTp, and consistent use of ITNs. During the past 12 months, more than 3,808 CHWs have been trained in IPTp promotion and delivery of an integrated package of services for the prevention of malaria in pregnancy. Over the past year, CHWs supported by PMI have promoted healthy motherhood through education and community sensitization by promoting ITN use and encouraging pregnant women to seek ANC services.

Plan and Justification
In 2014, an estimated 2.5 million SP tablets are needed to protect approximately 574,433 pregnant women expected to attend ANC clinics (80% of all pregnant women) and ensure a buffer stock of 25% for the 93 malaria-endemic health districts where MIP interventions are a part of the malaria prevention and control strategy. Global Fund will provide 43% of the SP need for IPTp in 2014 and ensure delivery to the district level. The *Service de Santé de District* (SSD or District Health Office) is responsible for assigning the estimated amount of SP needed by each CSB. CSB staff or community members are responsible for transporting the SP from the District Health Office to their local CSB. Additionally, the Global Fund NSA grant will provide funding to introduce SP among private and NGO providers and purchase SP for this sector, although distribution strategies have not yet been identified. Resources needed to procure the estimated

3.5 million SP tablets (approximately 583,000 treatments) needed for 2015 have not been secured. PMI will continue to encourage pregnant women to attend ANC services and request SP for IPTp. Since providing commodities to CSBs is restricted, in order to extend its reach to pregnant women, PMI will support distribution of SP for approximately 300 NGO and FBO clinics that are currently part of a USAID Maternal Child Health program network to expand IPTp to the private sector.

Challenges, opportunities, threats

Due to the USG suspension of direct support to the GoM since March 2009, PMI and other donors have not been able to support ANC services at CSBs. Despite the high reported rate of ANC attendance and relatively early attendance during the course of the pregnancy (2008-2009 DHS), IPTp uptake remains low. Results from the 2011 MIS reports reported that only 22% of pregnant women took two doses of SP for IPTp among the 93 IPTp targeted districts. It is unclear what obstacles are responsible for the poor uptake of IPTp. Stock-outs may not be the main obstacle. Inadequate supervision, lack of refresher training, and staffing shortages have been reported; these may be factors in limiting progress in IPTp implementation. Furthermore, some women attend ANC services at private clinics which do not regularly promote IPTp. In response to the reported low uptake of SP for IPTp, the NMCP, with partners, has employed alternative strategies such as using CHWs to deliver targeted messages for the prevention of malaria in pregnancy to pregnant women and encouraging them to attend ANC early and often and demand IPTp during their visits. CHWs also play an important role in planning, organizing, and conducting health promotion outreach activities, including IPTp for pregnant women, during the biannual mother and child health campaign weeks.

Currently, the new WHO guidelines for improved IPTp uptake have not been incorporated into the national malaria strategy. Due to limitations in providing direct support to the Government, PMI cannot provide technical assistance to support national policy change.

In addition, low-dose folic acid supplements will be procured by PMI for distribution by CHWs at the community level. This will serve as another opportunity to encourage early and regular ANC attendance by pregnant women and ensure uncompromised effectiveness of SP as folic acid in doses higher than 1mg can compromise the effectiveness of SP when given together.

Proposed activities with FY 2014 funding ($225,000)

1. Procure SP: PMI will procure SP for 300 private /NGO & FBO health facilities. ($15,000)

2. Procure low-dose folic acid and iron: PMI will procure low-dose folic acid/iron supplements for distribution to pregnant women by CHWs. ($10,000)

3. Community-based promotion of MIP service: Support community-based BCC promotion for uptake of ITNs and IPTp at ANC clinics. ($200,000)

4. Case management: Diagnostics

NMCP/PMI Objectives

The national policy on malaria case management, including diagnosis, states that all malaria cases should be confirmed parasitologically. Confirmation using RDTs was introduced by the MoH starting mid-2006 and reached all primary health care facilities by the end of 2008, along with the introduction of ACTs. If RDTs are not available, treatment with an ACT should be given based on clinical diagnosis, after eliminating all other causes of fever. In 2010, the national integrated community case management (iCCM) curriculum was revised to include RDT testing of all fever cases among children under five managed by CHWs.

Under the 2013–2017 National Strategic Plan, the goal in the control/consolidation phase is to correctly diagnose and treat at least 95% of malaria cases seen at public health facilities and at least 80% of all fever cases among children under five years old seen by CHWs. In pre-elimination areas, the goal is to correctly diagnose and treat 100% of malaria cases seen at public health facilities and >80% of all fever cases among children under five years old seen by CHWs.

Currently RDTs are used at all government primary health care facilities. The National Strategy calls for expansion of RDT use to hospital urgent care and outpatient clinic settings and to the private sector. The NMCP, with support from Global Fund, trained over 1,000 private providers in the national case management policy, which includes the use of RDTs to confirm all suspect malaria cases. To date, some FBO- and NGO-supported clinics have implemented the policy in collaboration with district health authorities and are supplied free ACTs and RDTs in return for providing standard monthly reports.

Progress during the last 12 months

With FY 2012 and FY 2013 funds, PMI procured RDTs for CHWs and FBO and NGO facilities. PMI also supported ongoing training, supervision, and use of RDTs by CHWs. PMI collaborated with the largest network of FBO and NGO primary health care clinics in Madagascar, promoted correct case management according to the national guidelines, and trained staff from an estimated 147 health facilities. The FBO and NGO staff were trained in stock management, recording, and reporting.

Plan and justification

PMI will continue to procure RDTs for the community level and NGO and FBO health centers. In addition, PMI will continue to support refresher training for CHWs and strengthen technical supportive supervision. This will occur in all districts supported by USAID bilateral agreements (this figure used to be 93 partial districts but is now is actually full coverage of 72 districts).

Challenges, opportunities, threats

Reliable data on the consumption of ACTs and RDTs at the community level is limited. Commodity needs are calculated based on morbidity estimates. Additionally, there is limited funding to purchase antibiotics and oral rehydration salts to treat pneumonia and diarrhea as part of iCCM. Ongoing stock procurement and management, to ensure a steady supply of RDTs and ACTs to all CHWs, CBOs, and FBOs, remains a challenge for Madagascar.

In additional to iCCM, several partners are working with CHWs to implement other interventions including child growth monitoring and nutrition programs, community directly observed treatment for tuberculosis, water and sanitation, and family planning programs. Coordination is challenging across different programs and partners, leading to incomplete geographic coverage in some areas and duplication of services in other areas. Efforts have been made to standardize the training curriculum, data recording, and reporting tools; however, there are several implementation challenges including: ensuring adequate CHW starter kits and ongoing medication stocks, and providing adequate technical supervision and oversight. CHW incentives have not been standardized and coordination among partners needs improvement. The national community health policy is currently being revised and an implementation guide is being developed to help provide guidance. The policy and guide will provide a basis to coordinate community health service provision among different programs and partners.

Gap analysis
Based on limited consumption data, it is estimated that each CHW trained in RDT use will require a starter pack of 40 RDTs and will use on average 12 RDTs per month for suspect malaria cases in children under five in their communities. We anticipate around 10,000 CHWs in PMI-supported programs will be using RDTs to diagnose malaria by the end of 2013.

Table 7: RDT gap analysis

Calendar Year	2013	2014	2015
RDT needs			
Public health facilities	1,613,291	1,433,562	1,242,504
Community-level needs	3,743,792	3,326,715	2,883,347
Private sector needs			
Epidemic stock	267,854	238,014	206,293
Safety stock for 2013	1,339,271		
Total RDT needs	6,964,208	4,998,291	4,332,143
RDT sources – supply			
Global Fund and UNITAID	3,236,000	3,820,000	4,332,143
PMI	1,000,000	1,178,291	
Total Estimated RDT Supply	4,236,000	4,998,291	4,332,143
RDT Gap	2,728,208	0	0

Proposed activities with FY 2014 funding ($4,338,650)

1. *Procure RDTs*: Purchase approximately 2.25 million RDTs (at an estimated cost of $0.80 per RDT); including RDTs for iCCM and for NGO and FBO clinics. This procurement will cover some of the iCCM RDT gap. Gloves and safety boxes for sharps disposal will also be procured to ensure biosafety and personal protection when using RDTs. *($2,302,650)*

2. *Refresher training and strengthening, M&E, and routine supervision of CHWs*: PMI funding will provide support for refresher training in all aspects of iCCM, strengthening M&E, and providing routine supervision of CHWs on the appropriate use of RDTs and treatment with ACTs. Funding will support at least 10,000 CHWs, in USAID districts. *($2,000,000)*

3. *Support for two Malaria Peace Corps Volunteers (PCVs)*: PMI, through implementing partners, will continue to support the Peace Corps-PMI collaboration by funding two third-year Peace Corps Volunteers. These Malaria Volunteers will focus on implementation, monitoring, and reporting of case management including iCCM activities at the commune level. Funding will include housing, and equipment costs. *($24,000)*

4. *Technical assistance*: Support one U.S. Centers for Disease Control and Prevention (CDC) technical assistance trip for diagnostics implementation at community level. *($12,000)*

5. Pharmaceutical and Commodity Management

NMCP/PMI Objectives
Public Sector: The 2013–2017 National Strategic Plan objectives for districts in the control/consolidation phase are to ensure that at least 95% of public health facilities have no more than one week of stock outs of RDTs, ACTs, SP, and routine ITNs in the proceeding three months. For districts in the pre-elimination phase, the objective is zero stock outs and the goal is to establish a functional routine quality control system in each pre-elimination phase district.

Madagascar Central Medical Stores (SALAMA), the national central purchasing agency, is responsible for procuring essential medicines and medical consumables for use in the public sector and a portion of the private sector and ensuring their distribution to the district level.

The drug supply system is based on a push system down to the districts. Delivery to CSBs is not clearly defined, combining the pull and push systems under the management of the *Médécin Inspecteur*. The absence of a clear scheme leads to frequent stock-outs. At the district level, the district pharmaceutical depots are the intermediary points in the public sector supply chain. They are managed primarily by NGOs under a contract with the MoH through the Department of Pharmacies, Laboratories, and Traditional Medicine and they sell to the health facility pharmacies. All medicines dispensed at public health facilities are sold with a mark-up of approximately 35% of the SALAMA price.

The free distribution of malaria commodities through the public sector has resulted in parallel procurement and distribution channels to the district level. There are also different channels for distributing antimalarial medicines and products within districts. Free and donated malaria commodities are received and managed by the District Health Office, while the products from SALAMA are managed by the district pharmaceutical depots. In both cases, CSBs are responsible for the collection and transportation of their supplies from the district level to their respective facilities. This limits the quantities that most of them can transport at any one time, as they primarily rely on public transportation. Furthermore, some CSB are inaccessible for 4-6 months of the year during the rainy season, thus requiring advanced planning to ensure a reliable supply of health commodities. An alternative supply channel proposed in the NSA II Grant application is that the CSB become the supply point for the community level, as of October 2013.

An assessment of the national pharmaceutical management capacity in 2008 highlighted the following constraints: (1) lack of trained pharmacists in public pharmacies; (2) insufficient pharmaceutical policies and guidelines; (3) low capacity and inadequate human resources for pharmaceutical management in the health-care system; (4) multiple vertical programs lacking integration and coordination; and (5) logistics and distribution challenges at the peripheral level. These problems still exist.

Private sector: The Global Fund-supported highly-subsidized ACTIpal® (the socially-marketed ACT for children under five years old; approximately $0.05 per treatment) is distributed to CHWs through various NGOs, private sector pharmacies, pharmacy depots, and private doctors, by private pharmaceutical wholesalers or by those contracted by Population Services International (PSI), the principal recipient for Global Fund grants. In addition to ACTs, CHWs also dispense other medicines subsidized under a social marketing model financed by USAID. This includes oral re-hydration salts plus zinc tablets (approximately $0.22) for the treatment of diarrhea among children under five years old; cotrimoxazole tablets (approximately $0.09), and cotrimoxazole oral suspension (approximately $0.32) for the treatment of uncomplicated pneumonia. PSI determines the profit margin at which these items are sold to the consumers by private providers. However, the profit margin gained by the CHWs is quite small, approximately $0.02-$0.11 per product sold. PMI contributes to this parallel system by procuring and distributing commodities and by providing technical assistance to support the CHWs programs. The CHWs are also trained to provide maternal, newborn, and child health services, including reproductive health counseling, family planning services, nutrition assessments, and treatment for pneumonia and diarrhea.

An active distribution system of antimalarial exists in the commercial private sector, particularly in urban areas with at least three local manufacturers who import finished antimalarial drugs for repackaging and sales. There are approximately 33 wholesalers, 200 private pharmacies, and 2,000 pharmacy depots.

Quality Assurance: The *Agence de Médicament de Madagascar* (AMM), which includes the National Medicines Quality Control Laboratory, is responsible for testing most pharmaceutical products destined for use in the country and products already on the market. The medicines quality monitoring program is designed to help the national drug authority to detect substandard and counterfeit medicines and take immediate action to remove such medicines from the market. Prior to the *coup d'état* in 2009, with USG support, the agency established seven peripheral minilab testing sites where samples of antimalarials are regularly collected and tested using portable quality testing kits. An additional 15 kits were procured in 2012 with the Affordable Medicines Facility – malaria (AMFm) funding, thus fulfilling the goal of expanding drug quality testing sites to the 22 regional reference hospitals in Madagascar. The original plan was to have central level laboratory analysis conducted every three months; however, limited funding only allows for testing every six months.

Progress during the last 12 months
PMI continues to support the distribution of ACTs and RDTs via CHWs to the communities located in fokontany that are at least five kilometers to the nearest public health facility. As of April 2013, more than 10,000 CHWs were receiving malaria commodities and support from PMI

via this parallel supply system. PMI will continue to support RDT distribution to these CHWs trained in iCCM. To date the total number of supply points is approximately 933 nationwide with the new Integrated Social Marketing Project, which will be funded by USAID. The goal is to establish a total of 1,200 supply points.

Plans and justification
PMI and other USG funding streams will continue to support the supply chain and distribution of malaria commodities to the community level using the existing parallel system. PMI will continue to work towards the integration of malaria activities at the community level across the country.

Challenges, opportunities, and threats
One challenge associated with the USG restriction on working with the GoM is PMI's inability to respond quickly to malaria outbreaks, as the CHW distribution system is completely separate from the public distribution system, and there is limited flexibility in distributing RDTs and ACTs to the CSBs. In the event of future epidemic response needs, the USAID Mission and PMI will work with the State Department to advocate use of PMI resources, including malaria commodities, to respond to emergencies in a timely and appropriate manner.

Another challenge with the parallel supply chain system is related to the forecasting and quantification of malaria medicines, with other donors. For example, recently Global Fund-financed malaria commodities were procured by three different Principal Recipients (PRs): one for the public sector, another for the community sector, and a third for both the public and community sectors. With the end of the Global Fund Round 7 grant that procured commodities for the community sector and the consolidation of the Global Fund commodities under one PR (*Unité de Gestion de Projet* or UGP) in the NSA-II, the nature of needs coordination is changing. The Global Fund Round 7 project to support socially marketed ACTs at the community level ends in September 2013. The NSA II will be covering community ACT needs and they will be managed and distributed to CHWs through the CSB. Careful coordination between the different supply systems will be essential to ensure a reliable supply chain at the community level and the long-term strategy agreed upon between the Global Fund and the Ministry of Health is to use the CSB as the main supply point for CHWs.

Avoiding stock-outs by ensuring that orders are placed with sufficient time for distribution and taking into account the issues of multiple supply chains has proven difficult. In addition, the sustainability of the resupply system, especially at the community level, is a challenge. The link between the CHWs and the primary health facility is weak, which limits the options CHWs have to resupply their commodities.

Proposed activities with FY 2014 funding ($300,000)

1. *Strengthen the supply chain for malaria commodities at the community level:* PMI will ensure the continuous supply of RDTs and ACTs via supportive supervision to support the timely diagnosis and treatment of malaria at the community level. This activity will be co-funded with other USAID Health Office programs. *($300,000)*

6. Treatment

NMCP/PMI Objectives

AS/AQ combination therapy is the first-line antimalarial treatment in Madagascar, and artemether/lumefantrine (AL) is considered as an alternative therapy for those that cannot tolerate AS/AQ due to side effects.

The 2013–2017 National Strategic Plan recommends intravenous artesunate for the treatment of severe malaria in Madagascar. This change will be phased in based on available funding to support the transition from quinine to artesunate. Pre-referral rectal artesunate will be piloted and evaluated and eventually phased in at both primary health care centers and as appropriate at the community level. In pre-elimination zones, a single dose of primaquine (0.75mg/kg) will be added to AS/AQ for uncomplicated falciparum malaria as an antigametocyte medicine.

Progress during last 12 months

PMI provides support to two bilateral projects that focus on community delivery of health services that include integrated case management of malaria, diarrhea, and pneumonia by CHWs (iCCM). Global Fund and UNICEF also provide significant support to the NMCP and the MoH for this approach. When fully operational, PMI implementing partners will reach about two-thirds of the more than 1,500 communes across the 72 districts in the country, supporting around 10,000 CHWs. Across all partners, over 35,000 CHWs have been trained in integrated community case management since 2009. In 2011 and 2012, an additional 941 CHWs were recruited and trained to replace CHWs lost to routine attrition. CHWs played an important role in assessing, diagnosing, and treating over 30,000 cases of fever among children under 5 years old over the past 12 months.

Figure 5: CHWs in Madagascar

○ MAHEFA
○ New PHC

Plans and Justification

PMI will continue to collaborate with the Global Fund and UNICEF to expand iCCM throughout Madagascar so that all children with fever are promptly diagnosed and treated at community level. PMI has expanded its coverage of CHWs in remote areas of the West and North of the country, complementing areas already covered in the East and South.

PMI will continue to procure RDTs for use by CHWs and approximately 300 FBO and NGO private sector health facilities.

Gap Analysis

Table 8: Gap analysis for ACTs 2012-2014

Calendar Year	2013	2014	2015
Public health facilities	504,153	447,988	388,283
Community-level needs	652,800	580,075	502,765
Private sector needs	301,411	267,832	232,137
Epidemic stock (5%)	57,848	51,403	44,552
Buffer stock (25%)	289,238		
Total ACT needs	**1,805,450**	**1,347,298**	**1,167,737**
Global Fund	1,871,125	367,086	
Private sector	301,411	267,832	232,137
PMI	0	50,000	0
Total Estimated ACT Supply	2,172,536	684,918	232,137
ACT Gap	**367,086**	**662,380**	**935,600**
ACT in Global Fund NSA II Proposal	367,086	662,380	935,600

The estimated ACT needs were calculated using both the morbidity method and annual incidence of fever calculation method and produced results similar to those shown in the above table. Currently stock reporting from health facilities and the community level is incomplete. Available monthly consumption data and reporting on stock-outs is of variable quality and it is not possible to estimate national needs based on the consumption method.

The remaining ACT gap in the table above has been included in the current Global Fund NSA II funding proposal, which is under review as of April 2013. However, PMI remains willing to conduct an emergency procurement of ACTs if necessary to prevent stock outs of ACTs at the community level.

Challenges, opportunities, and threats

As discussed above in the diagnostics section, key challenges include commodity management and ensuring a regular reliable supply of RDTs and ACTs to all levels of the health system, especially to the highly decentralized community level, and improving coordination of iCCM with other community health programs and among implementing partners and stakeholders.

Madagascar was selected as one of nine pilot countries to expand ACTs to the private sector through the Global Fund Affordable Medicines Facility – malaria (AMFm). Madagascar imported the first subsidized ACTs in early 2011. The project has resulted in increased demand and sale of ACTs on the private market at a cost to consumers of $0.24-$0.48 per treatment especially in pharmacies and medicine depots.[14] By the end of 2011, ACTs had the leading market share in private health facilities and pharmacies. Furthermore, the availability of ACTs played a key role during the response to a malaria epidemic in the southeast in 2012. Public

---

[14] Tracking survey April 2012, ACTWatch Outlet survey 2011

sector ACTs were stocked out and the GoM worked with partners to purchase readily available ACTs at the central and local level from first-line buyers to respond quickly to the epidemic. The shift in Global Fund focus away from the AMFm will have consequences in Madagascar, potentially increasing the demand for ACTs in the public health facilities and/or returning to increased use of non-ACT antimalarial still readily available in the private market.

Proposed Activities with FY 2014 funding ($12,000)

1. *Technical assistance to support community case management.* Support for one CDC TA to support the community case management of malaria. (*$12,000*)

7. Behavior Change Communication

The Madagascar MIS conducted between March and May 2011 collected information on knowledge and use of ITNs and knowledge on modes of malaria transmission, prevention, and treatment. MIS results show that during the 12 months preceding the survey, 7 out of 10 mothers (70%) were informed about distribution of free nets in ANC clinics, and 2 out of 5 (42%) received a message on where to buy a bed net. Close to two-thirds (64%) were informed about how to hang their bed nets, 65% were informed about how to take care of the nets, and slightly over two-thirds (67%) received the message on the benefits of ITN use. Knowledge of ITN use and benefits was found to be higher compared to knowledge of other key preventive behaviors promoted with PMI support, despite the high knowledge about transmission of malaria through mosquito bites. Among women aged 15–49 with children under five or who were pregnant, 73% cited fever as the main symptom of malaria, and 70% cited mosquito bites as the means of transmission. On the treatment side, only 1 in 5 (19%) cited AS/AQ and only 10% cited ACTIpal as the most effective antimalarial drugs available for treating their children with malaria symptoms. Also among women with children under five, 58% knew a place where to buy an antimalarial. With regards to malaria in pregnancy, only 14% of pregnant women or mothers of children under five years old think it is important to take IPTp; however, 71% know they should go to the health facility during pregnancy for ANC and receive a preventive antimalarial. MIS findings show clearly the need to invest into more targeted BCC to increase IPTp uptake and appropriate care-seeking.

The 2011 MIS results showed that more than half of children with fever (56%) do not seek treatment from skilled providers. CHWs will also educate community members in recognizing danger signs of severe malaria that require immediate attention. CHWs will be tasked to conduct door-to-door visits to conduct interpersonal communication with caregivers, especially with mothers, on the necessity to seek treatment at the onset of fever, without delay.

Malaria messaging will focus on rural areas and will include community-based interpersonal communication, skits and dramas, mobile video unit shows, and radio spots. The 2011 MIS results showed IRS coverage of 79% in targeted districts – the coverage is lower than expected and attributed to households refusing IRS – especially in extension districts and the South, where insecurity prevented IRS. BCC will focus on community sensitization for these zones in particular. BCC messages for ITNs will promote correct use, discourage inappropriate use, encourage correct ITN care (washing, storage) to help promote ITN maintenance over time, and encourage people to use their new nets and replace old nets that are past their effective life span or in a state of disrepair.

Plan and Justification

Targeted and general BCC activities will be implemented to mobilize traditional and religious community leaders and civic organizations to promote malaria prevention and control, with the aim of reaching pre-elimination status, particularly in the Central Highlands, and consolidating control measures in the rest of the country. These activities include promoting the use of ITNs by the general population and by pregnant women and children under five in particular, promoting community acceptance of IRS, early and regular antenatal clinic attendance to ensure uptake of IPTp, and prompt diagnosis and treatment of malaria.

To complement these mass media efforts, interpersonal communication and community-based behavior change interventions will be implemented through NGOs and CHWs. The CHWs will provide outreach to families to convey malaria prevention awareness messages and to teach personal preventive behaviors through participatory radio listening groups, small group education sessions, and home puppets, which are popular in Madagascar. Skits and dramas will also be used to convey messages and promote behaviors. Use of interpersonal communication approaches will be prioritized over the use of mass media, aiming for approximately 70% of BCC funding to be interpersonal communication in communities where awareness of malaria is high enough for this approach to be effective.

PMI's support to BCC activities will continue to be aimed towards empowering individuals and families to prevent and treat malaria correctly. This will be accomplished primarily through PMI's continued support of CHWs to encourage pregnant women and women with children needing immunizations to visit ANC and EPI clinics to request free ITNs under the continuous distribution schemes that were initiated in 2013. Also, CHWs and NGOs will support the nationwide, biannual mother and child health weeks, which provide catch-up immunizations, vitamin A supplements, deworming medicine and, at times, free ITNs for children under five years of age. By providing folic acid/iron supplements to pregnant women, CHWs will have yet another opportunity to promote ANC attendance to receive IPTp and ITNs. The CHWs involved with distribution of socially marketed products will educate local residents on proper care and use of ITNs and on the necessity of prompt diagnosis and correct treatment with ACTs, with special emphasis on children under five at the household level.

PMI will continue support for the National Strategic Plan goal to implement integrated community case management of malaria, pneumonia, and diarrheal diseases in all districts.

Challenges, opportunities, threats

Due to the political constraints related to working with the Government of Madagascar (GoM) since March 2009, PMI and a few other donors have not been able to directly support malaria control activities in the public health sector making opportunities to implement BCC activities to promote uptake of malaria intervention limited. PMI, along with other development partners, have employed alternative strategies such as using CHWs to deliver targeted messages to promote increased uptake of malaria interventions.

Proposed activities with FY 2014 funding ($480,000)

1. Implementation of community-based malaria activities: Support the implementation of community case management of malaria through CHWs, using integrated malaria messaging including the four key messages related to correct use of ITNs, acceptance of IRS where applicable, preventing malaria among pregnant women, and early and prompt care seeking. Special efforts will be deployed for the uptake of IPTp and appropriate care seeking. Funds will support grants to local NGOs that provide technical support and supervision to the network of CHWs. *($300,000)*

2. Support for malaria BCC activities to create demand for prevention and case management in the general populace, including ITNs, ACT promotion and early treatment-seeking behavior. ($150,000)

3. Support Malaria Peace Corps Volunteers: Funding will continue to support a PCV coordinator, who will facilitate malaria BCC activity implementation among Madagascar Peace Corps Volunteers. Funds will also be used to support malaria training for all PCVs which will be integrated with other mid-service and in-service trainings. *($30,000)*

8. Capacity Building and Health Systems Strengthening

Due to the USG restrictions in Madagascar, PMI funds are unable to directly support capacity building of NMCP staff or strengthening of the health system. PMI is poised to provide support in the future and will conduct a reprogramming exercise once USG restrictions are lifted.

9. Monitoring and Evaluation

NMCP/PMI Objectives

The Madagascar M&E strategy for malaria has been developed to facilitate the collection, analysis, and quality assurance of data from health centers, partners, communities, sentinel sites, and household surveys. A comprehensive National M&E Plan was written for 2008–2012 and has recently been updated for the period 2013–2017.

The 2013–2017 National Strategy for Epidemic Surveillance and Response objectives include:

For control and consolidation zones:
- 100% of epidemics are detected and controlled properly within 15 days
- Assure the quality of at least 80% of data reported from health facilities on malaria

For pre-elimination zones:
- 100% of epidemics are detected and controlled properly within 15 days
- Assure the quality of at least 90% of data reported from health facilities on malaria

Current M&E System: The current M&E system for malaria is comprised of: 1) the national health management information system (HMIS), which reports malaria cases and deaths monthly from health facilities; 2) a malaria-specific district-level surveillance system (originally for 36 epidemic-prone districts and weekly monitoring of confirmed malaria cases and deaths, currently covering only 28 districts; 3) an integrated fever sentinel surveillance system, which provides highly accurate and rapid reporting of data from individual sentinel health facilities; and 4) population-based surveys such as DHS and MIS. The national M&E plan calls for integration of community-based malaria surveillance information through CHWs, who diagnose and treat children under five years old with fever. The current system is fragmented, only partially functional, and is neither timely nor complete. Data collected through this system must be triangulated to assess progress in malaria prevention and case management. Additional M&E data are available, including insecticide resistance monitoring, therapeutic efficacy studies conducted approximately every two years (in 2006, in 2008–9, 2010, 2012), and pharmacovigilance monitoring. The table below summarizes some of the key monitoring and evaluation data for malaria in Madagascar, including national-level surveys, routine and specialized surveillance systems, and other data sources.

Table 9: Key Monitoring & Evaluation Data in Madagascar

Data Source	Year								
	2008	2009	2010	2011	2012	2013	2014	2015	2016
Household Surveys		DHS (08-09)	LLIN univ coverage campaign eval	MIS	MDG	MIS LLIN univ coverage campaign eval*		MIS	
Other Surveys	ACT outlet/ HH survey (ACT Watch)*		ACT outlet/ HH(?)/ drug quality survey (ACT Watch)*	CHW cross-sectional eval of performance					
Malaria Surveillance and routine system support[3]	RMA/ HMIS/ GMP database* Fever sentinel surv system IDSR*	RMA/ HMIS/ GMP database* Fever sentinel surv system IDSR* PNLP malaria sentinel surv*	RMA/ HMIS/ GMP database* Fever sentinel surv system IDSR* PNLP malaria sentinel surv*	RMA/ HMIS/ GMP database* Fever sentinel surv system IDSR* PNLP malaria sentinel surv*	RMA/ HMIS/ GMP database* Fever sentinel surv system IDSR* PNLP malaria sentinel surv*	RMA/ HMIS/ GMP database* Fever sentinel surv system IDSR* PNLP malaria sentinel surv* CHW surveillance pilot (IPM)	RMA/ HMIS/ GMP database*	RMA/ HMIS/ GMP database*	RMA/ HMIS/ GMP database*
Other Data Sources[4]	Ento monitoring TES* TRaC*	Ento monitoring	Ento monitoring Rapid Impact Assessmt TES* DSS* TRaC*	CHW program functionality assessmt (HCI) Ento monitoring DSS*	Ento monitoring LLIN durability eval CHW assessmt TES* DSS*	Ento monitoring LLIN durability Monitoring TES* DSS*	DSS*	DSS*	DSS*

* Not PMI-supported; TRaC supported by PSI; ACTWatch by ACTWatch/Bill and Melinda Gates Foundation via PSI; TES by Global Fund for AIDS, Tuberculosis, and Malaria; IDSR supported by WHO and other sources.

HMIS=Health management information system; TES=Therapeutic efficacy study; TRaC= Tracking Results Continuously ; DSS=Demographic surveillance system; RMA=*Rapport Mensuel des Activités*; GMP=Global Malaria Programme (of WHO)

Enhanced surveillance for Epidemic-Prone zones: The current epidemic surveillance monitoring system (*Postes Sentinelles de Surveillance* or Sentinel surveillance sites) was established in 1997 with 8 original districts. It was then increased to 12 and later expanded to cover 36 districts at risk for epidemics in the Central Highlands and South by 2005. At present, however, not all 36 districts have functioning systems. This system was established with support from Global Fund Round 3 and it initially supported 12 dedicated malaria surveillance staff working at the district level to report suspected and confirmed malaria cases weekly from all health facilities in their respective districts. The staff are trained in surveillance, data analysis, and interpretation of malaria epidemic investigation and response efforts; they are also provided with a motorcycle for transport and computers. District-level and central-level databases have been established and report suspect and confirmed malaria cases and deaths on a weekly basis. Data reported from these districts are generally of better quality and timelier than those from districts without dedicated malaria surveillance staff, which also rely on the general HMIS reporting system.

Multiple interruptions in financing due to administrative delays between grants and between phases have led to an interruption of funding to support dedicated surveillance staff. As a result, the system experienced a decline in data quality and a 100% turnover in the past five years. The system is being rebuilt and new staff were recruited and trained in 2011 and 2012. The system has been expanded to include an additional 33 districts, including the IRS extension districts (zone bordering the epidemic prone areas), and will be expanded nationwide to ensure epidemic surveillance and response capacity exists in all areas of Madagascar. Dedicated malaria surveillance staff provide invaluable support when the system is working, as demonstrated by the early detection, investigation, and management of malaria outbreaks, including sentinel surveillance site requests for assistance and mobilization of resources to respond to multiple malaria epidemics identified in 2012 and early 2013. In 2012, 33 alerts were identified and among those 5 were confirmed epidemics. In the first quarter of 2013, 15 districts reported alerts and four were confirmed focal epidemics. It will likely take another one to two years for the system to become fully functional, assuming resources can be found and trained staff retained. PMI does not currently provide financial support to the sentinel surveillance site system.

In addition to the above surveillance system, the NMCP has adopted the Malaria Early Warning System (MEWS) framework, which is functional and includes analysis of climate data for predicting epidemics. A fever surveillance system managed by *Institut Pasteur-Madagascar* (IPM) at 34 sentinel sites also provides weekly data on fever causes. During June 2013, the Roll Back Malaria partners convened a workshop to harmonize the various epidemic detection systems in Madagascar and update the country's epidemic detection and response guidelines.

A complementary fever surveillance system developed by the *Direction des Urgences et de la Lutte contre les Maladies Négligées, Direction de la veille sanitaire et de la surveillance epidemiologique,* the NMCP, and IPM is actively collecting data on fever cases from 34 sentinel CSB sites. These sites use syndromic surveillance coupled with confirmation by diagnostic testing to systematically classify all fever cases as a laboratory-confirmed malaria case, a suspected case of an outbreak-prone disease (i.e., arbovirus, influenza, malaria), or other fever.

In 2007, 13 sites were established in CSBs across four malaria epidemiological zones with support from World Bank. PMI began supporting these sites in FY 2008 and increased the number of sites to 15 in April 2010 using FY 2009 funding. Aggregate data on the number of fever cases is transmitted daily to the central level from each site using short message service phone technology, including demographic information, clinical symptoms, RDT results, and history of antimalarial treatment before clinical consultation. Weekly feedback on reported data is provided by IPM to the fever sentinel sites, and a monthly newsletter summarizing the reported cases and trends is distributed to the RBM partners and other stakeholders. Promptness of reporting and quality of data are very good, and the aggregate reports are received daily >95% of the time. On average, fewer than 5% of reports require correction of errors. In addition, reporting and analysis are comprehensive, timely, and complete and provide trends of confirmed cases of malaria since 2007. A once-yearly RDT quality control system for the sentinel sites has been established to monitor RDT quality, storage and use. During supervision visits, RDT storage areas are visited and the temperature of the storage area is taken. Health staff are observed performing RDTs over two days, and a second RDT, a microscopy slide, and dried blood spot are collected from each patient seen with a fever. Health staff are given feedback on RDT use and their RDT readings are compared to a control RDT and microscopy.

Several fever surveillance sites are also part of the network of IPM sites used in monitoring antimalarial drug efficacy and are undergoing activity integration to be more representative. First-line antimalarial drug (AS/AQ) efficacy monitoring is done every two years by IPM with funding provided by the Global Fund. The 2009 study conducted in Maevatanana showed 100% efficacy of AS/AQ; subsequent studies at two sites in 2010, Vatomandry and Miandriavazo, showed 98.8-100% efficacy.

Indicator reporting: Coverage data for malaria interventions and program indicators are captured from several sources. NMCP, in collaboration with WHO, has developed a central database that receives data from regional and district levels, which augment HMIS' routine reporting. District and regional staff have been trained on database utilization.

Compilation of malaria data reported through the HMIS is completed with the assistance of a data manager supported by Global Fund grants. All reports starting in 2008 have been entered into the central database and are available for use by the NMCP. The NMCP is developing a format for sharing program progress. The NMCP is planning to publish a quarterly bulletin that includes key malaria morbidity and mortality indicators. The NMCP has also recently created a website for sharing program information: http://www.pnlp-madagascar.mg.

The central M&E unit in the NMCP, consisting of an epidemiologist, an informatics expert, and data entry assistants, is currently supported by the Global Fund grants. The staff of the central M&E unit train regional staff and have created a network of 22 regional and 112 district malaria program-specific staff who assist in monitoring and supervision, data collection, and analysis. Sites are equipped with a computer and office equipment and use the same database as the central level.

As a result of recommendations from a Global Fund data quality assurance evaluation conducted in 2010, the NMCP began conducting routine data quality assessments every six months with the goal of identifying problems and monitoring and improving data quality. Findings are discussed and reviewed with RBM partners regularly. Recently data quality assessment has been incorporated into health facility supervision tool in order to continuously monitor and improve data quality. The new supervision tool will be used starting in mid-2013.

Household Surveys: The baseline national household survey for PMI is the 2008-2009 DHS. Follow-up national surveys include the 2011 MIS and a MIS in 2013. The 2013 MIS is underway as a key survey to show program results after implementation of the 2008-2012 National Strategic plan and the first phase (two years) of the three-year Global Fund National Strategic Application grant. In addition, a large household survey to measure progress toward the Millennium Development Goals (MDGs) in Madagascar was funded by UN partners and health donor partners, including PMI. The MDG survey was completed in January 2013 and replaces the 2013–14 DHS survey. Data entry is currently underway and preliminary results are expected in September 2013. Reprogrammed PMI FY 2012 funds ($300,000) supported the survey implementation and PMI staff worked with the steering committee to ensure key indicators were included and that the data and database are available for secondary analysis to inform the RBM/PMI impact evaluation planned in 2014. This household survey used a combination of two large standard household survey questionnaires: the DHS questionnaire and Living Standards Measurement Survey questionnaire.

Progress during the last 12 months

Sentinel Surveillance: PMI continues to support the fever surveillance sites. PMI started with support for 13 fever sentinel sites (FY 2008), and since then has added 2 sites for a total of 15 sites. The number of sites was increased without additional cost, and the per-site cost has actually gone down over the years due to increased efficiency. The sites are managed by IPM, a non-governmental organization that has consistently and reliably conducted quality-controlled fever and malaria case reporting to PMI for 15 sentinel sites. IPM reports detailed treatment and IPTp indicators from ten sites. IPM has funding from other donors and expanded the total number of functional sites to 34. Because of the ongoing political crisis limiting data access, the fever sentinel sites system is currently the only readily available source of timely malaria morbidity trend data available to PMI and USG. The fever sentinel site data have been used to detect and responds to potential epidemics in several regions of Madagascar in 2012 and 2013.

Community-based malaria surveillance: Reporting from CHWs is being integrated into the HMIS. In fall 2012, PMI supported an assessment of the CHW recording and reporting system and provided recommendations for how to streamline the system and integrate it into routine reporting.

Household Surveys: The MDG survey was completed in January 2013 and should provide updated malaria coverage indicators and a child mortality estimate. This survey was co-funded by PMI, which participated actively in the planning meetings and contributed to survey design and the analysis plan. Results from this survey will be used for child mortality estimates and to assess the progress in other child survival program indicators. The 2013 MIS will be used as the main source of malaria coverage results to be compared with the 2011 MIS and the baseline

2008-2009 DHS. The 2013 MIS, co-funded by PMI, will provide the second nationwide sample of parasitemia results in Madagascar.

Routine reporting: PMI has built upon the experiences of IPM in Madagascar and those from other countries to introduce the use of RDTs at the community level. A simplified system for reporting confirmed malaria cases was developed to capture data from communities. To date, reports are incomplete; however, as the system matures, this information will be available for monthly reporting to CSBs and also used for forecasting both ACT and RDT needs at the community level.

Plans and justifications
With FY 2014 funding, PMI will continue to support malaria surveillance and survey activities. PMI will continue to support fever sentinel site surveillance and also support impact evaluation methodology development and analysis. In addition, PMI will fund a new MIS planned for 2015.

Challenges, opportunities, threats
The political situation in Madagascar continues to present significant challenges for PMI. However, the limited capacity in the NMCP and health system cannot be addressed by PMI at this time. Moreover, recent malaria epidemic in the South and East highlight the precarious nature of the gains made in malaria control. Madagascar's geography results in limited access to health centers for the rural population. When capacity is built at the community level, the reach of malaria interventions can be expanded and their effectiveness increased.

More than 35,000 CHWs had been trained in community case management by December 2012. To date, community level reporting is neither complete nor timely and is of variable quality. In addition, the current HMIS database includes only partial reporting of cases (malaria, diarrhea, and pneumonia) from the community level and the information is not available centrally. Future PMI support will focus on efforts to improve technical supervision, CHW performance, and strengthen reporting.

Although working with community-based organizations and community workers as well as FBOs can be used to expand malaria control activities, the ability of these organizations to absorb the resources quickly and be able to monitor their activities appropriately may be limited. Implementing partners without sufficient technical capacity for program monitoring will need guidance from PMI to ensure that an appropriate M&E strategy is in place. PMI will continue to leverage the RBM partnership and other sources of funding to improve surveillance systems and the quality of malaria program data.

Proposed activities with FY 2014 funding ($512,000)

1. *Continued support for 15 fever sentinel sites* to monitor the impact of program interventions on malaria morbidity within the same catchment areas. Develop a model for timely and high-quality community-level malaria surveillance to be implemented in geographic zones moving towards pre-elimination. *($300,000)*

2. *Continued support for community-based malaria surveillance:* to implement community based surveillance activities in zones that are progressing towards pre-elimination to strengthen epidemic detection and response through CHWs. *(See Case Management Section)*

3. *Support preparation for the 2015 MIS*: PMI will contribute to supporting the 2015 MIS. PMI funding will complement Global Fund funding. *($200,000)*

4. *Technical assistance:* One CDC TDY and one USAID TDY for the support of PMI Madagascar M&E activities, including support for the impact evaluation. The USAID TDY will be centrally funded. *($12,000)*

10. Staffing and Administration

Two health professionals serve as Resident Advisors (RAs) to oversee PMI in Madagascar, one representing CDC and one representing USAID. In addition, two Malagasy staff, a Senior Public Health Malaria Specialist and a Program Management Assistant work as part of the team. All PMI staff members are part of a single inter-agency team led by the USAID Health Officer, who has been delegated that authority by the USAID Mission Director. The PMI team shares responsibility for development and implementation of PMI strategies and work plans, coordination with national authorities, management of collaborating agencies, and supervision of day-to-day activities. Candidates for resident advisor positions (whether initial hires or replacements) will be evaluated and/or interviewed jointly by USAID and CDC, and both agencies will be involved in hiring decisions, with the final decision made by the individual agency.

The PMI professional staff work together and oversee all technical and administrative aspects of PMI in Madagascar, including finalizing details of project design, implementing malaria prevention and case management activities, monitoring and evaluation of outcomes and impact, reporting of results, and providing guidance to PMI partners.

The PMI lead in country is the USAID Mission Director. The two PMI resident advisors, one from USAID and one from CDC, report to the Senior USAID Health Officer for day-to-day leadership, and work together as a part of a single interagency team. The technical expertise housed in Atlanta and Washington guides PMI programmatic efforts and thus overall technical guidance for both RAs falls to the PMI staff in Atlanta and Washington. Since the CDC resident advisor is a CDC employee (CDC USDD-38), responsibility for completing official performance reviews lies with CDC supervisor based in Atlanta who is expected to rely upon input from PMI staff across the two agencies that work closely day in and day out with the CDC RA and thus best positioned to comment on the RA's performance.

All technical activities are undertaken in close coordination with the MoH/NMCP and other national and international partners, including the WHO, UNICEF, the Global Fund, World Bank, and the private sector including NGOs and FBOs.

Locally-hired staff to support PMI activities either in Ministries or in USAID will be approved by the USAID Mission Director. Because of the need to adhere to specific country policies and USAID accounting regulations, any transfer of PMI funds directly to Ministries or host governments will need to be approved by the USAID Mission Director and Controller, in addition to the PMI Coordinator.

Proposed USG component: ($1,118,400)

1. In-country PMI staff salaries, benefits, travel, and other PMI administrative costs: Continued support for two PMI (CDC and USAID) Resident Advisors and FSN staff members to oversee activities supported by PMI in Madagascar. Additionally, these funds will support pooled USAID Madagascar Mission staff and mission-wide assistance from which PMI benefits. *($1,118,400)*

Table 1: President's Malaria Initiative - Madagascar (FY 2014) Budget Breakdown by Partner

Partner	Geographical Area	Activity	Budget ($)	%
DELIVER	93 districts	Procure 2.8 million LLINs for the 2015 mass distribution campaign	$10,249,950	50%
	93 districts	Technical assistance for procurement and supply chain management	$300,000	
	Nationwide	Support Malaria Peace Corps Volunteer	$12,000	
	93 districts	Procure SP	$15,000	
	93 districts	Iron supplement and low-dose folic acid	$10,000	
	Nationwide	Procure RDTs for malaria case management	$2,302,650	
PSI	93 districts	Distribution of the LLINs for the 2015 LLIN Campaign	$2,800,000	13%
	Nationwide	Strengthen supply chain for malaria commodities to the community level	$300,000	
	Nationwide	BCC to create demand for malaria prevention and control commodities and health behaviors.	$150,000	
	Nationwide (epidemic)	Distribution of LLINs for epidemic response per the national plan	$50,000	
TBD	93 districts	Undertake activities to increase the survivorship and durability of LLINs in Madagascar	$50,000	22%
	15 geographic areas	IRS in 15 geographic areas	$5,131,000	
	9 surveillance sites	IRS entomological monitoring	$225,000	
	Nationwide	Support preparation for a large national household survey (MIS 2015)	$200,000	
USAID	Nationwide	Technical assistance to LLIN activities	$0	2%
	Nationwide	Technical assistance to support M&E activities	$0	
	Nationwide	In country staffing and administration costs	$618,400	
CDC/IAA	Nationwide	Technical assistance to LLIN activities	$12,000	2%
	9 surveillance sites	Technical assistance to PMI IRS activities	$24,000	
	Nationwide	Technical assistance to diagnostic activities	$12,000	
	Nationwide	Technical assistance to support community case management	$12,000	

	Nationwide	Technical assistance to support M&E activities	$12,000	
	Nationwide	In country staffing and administration costs	$500,000	
New RFA PHC Project	~48 districts	Community based promotion of MIP services	$100,000	5%
	~48 districts	Refresher training and supervision of community case management	$1,000,000	
	Nationwide	Support for Malaria Peace Corps Volunteers	$12,000	
	~48 districts	Implementation of community-based malaria activities through integrated CCM interventions through NGOs/FBOs	$200,000	
MAHEFA	~32 districts	Community based promotion of MIP services	$100,000	5%
	~32 districts	Refresher training and supervision of community case management	$1,000,000	
	Nationwide	Support for Malaria Peace Corps Volunteers	$12,000	
	~32 districts	Implementation of community-based malaria activities through integrated CCM interventions through NGOs/FBOs	$100,000	
Peace Corps	Nationwide	Support to malaria Peace Corps Volunteers	$30,000	0%
IPM	Nationwide	Continue support for 15 fever sentinel sites of the fever surveillance system	$300,000	1%
	Nationwide	Entomological investigations in response to outbreaks of malaria	$80,000	
Total			**$25,920,000**	**100%**

Table 2: President's Malaria Initiative - Madagascar
FY 2014 Planned Obligations

Proposed Activity	Mechanism	Total Budget	Commodities	Geographic area	Description of Activity
ITNs					
Procure 2.8 million LLINs for the 2015 mass distribution campaign	DELIVER	$10,249,950	$10,249,950	93 districts	Procure ~2.8 million LLINs @ $3.6 per LLIN to contribute to the mass distribution campaign planned for 2015 and support for TA.
Technical assistance for procurement and supply chain management	DELIVER	$300,000	$0	93 districts	Administrative and technical support for PSM.
Distribution of the LLINs for the 2015 LLIN Campaign	PSI	$2,800,000	$0	93 districts	Funding for logistics, BCC activities, training and M&E for the 2015 LLIN Mass Distribution Campaign.
Undertake activities to increase the survivorship and durability of LLINs in Madagascar	TBD	$50,000	$0	93 districts	Year 2 of the LLIN durability monitoring of net distributed in 2014. This activity builds on the various LLIN durability studies in several PMI countries, along with the durability monitoring undertaken in Madagascar in 2012.
Support Malaria Peace Corps Volunteer	DELIVER	$12,000	$0	Nationwide	Support to a third-year PCV to work on implementation of malaria interventions. Funding will support 1 PCV nested with the implementing partner and will include housing, transport and equipment.
Technical assistance to LLIN activities	USAID	$0	$0	Nationwide	One USAID TDY to provide technical support for LLINs activities. *(Funding included in core budget)*
Technical assistance to LLIN activities	CDC/IAA	$12,000	$0	Nationwide	One CDC TDY to provide technical support for LLIN activities.
Epidemic Preparedness and Response					
Distribution of LLINs for epidemic response per the national plan	PSI	$50,000	$0	Nationwide (epidemic)	Distribution of LLINs in response to emergencies and/or epidemics

58

Activity	Mechanism	Budget	Budget	Target	Illustrative activities
Subtotal		$50,000	$0		
Subtotal: ITNs		$13,473,950	$10,249,950		
IRS					
IRS in 15 geographic areas	TBD	$5,131,000	$2,000,000	15 geographic areas	Conduct targeted IRS based on stratification of PMI supported zones (Central Highlands, Fringe, extension south and west). Cost of $18 per structure to cover approximately 396,000 structures. IRS implementation will following the national strategy goal of pre-elimination using targeted IRS, and includes the procurement of insecticides (including additional funding for insecticide rotation as a resistance management strategy), personal protective equipment, training, environmental component, BCC, M&E and operations.
IRS entomological monitoring	TBD	$225,000	$0	9 surveillance sites	Conduct comprehensive IRS-related vector surveillance, assess resistance and other indicators of IRS impact: vector taxonomy and density, and insecticide decay rates. Assumption of $25k per site per year, with 2 sites in 4 transmission zones, plus a additional control site where IRS will not be implemented.
Entomological investigations in response to outbreaks of malaria	IPM	$80,000	$0	Nationwide	Support epidemic response and entomologic investigations of alerts.
Technical assistance to PMI IRS activities	CDC/IAA	$24,000	$0	9 surveillance sites	Two CDC TDYs to provide support for insecticide resistance & IRS monitoring.
Subtotal: IRS		$5,460,000	$2,000,000		
MIP					
Procure SP	DELIVER	$15,000	$15,000	93 districts	Purchase of SP for ~ 300 NGO/FBOs.
Iron supplement and low-dose folic acid	DELIVER	$10,000	$10,000	93 districts	Purchase low dose folic acid and iron for distribution to pregnant women by CHWs.
Community-based promotion of MIP service	New RFA PHC Project	$100,000	$0	~48 districts	Support community-based BCC promotion for uptake of ITNs and IPTp at ANCs.
	MAHEFA	$100,000	$0	~32 districts	

Activity	Implementer	Location	Budget	Budget	Notes
Subtotal: IPTp			$225,000	$25,000	
Case Management					
Diagnostics					
Procure RDTs for malaria case management	DELIVER	Nationwide	$2,302,650	$2,302,650	Purchase ~2.25M RDTs: for X.XM CCM + Xk RDTs for FBO/NGO clinics. Procurement will also include procurement of gloves for both CHWs + FBOs, and safety boxes for CHWs. Assumes cost of $.80 per RDT; $.22 per pair of gloves @ 1 pair per RDT; and $.45 per safely box @ 34k for CHW.
Refresher training and supervision of community case management	New RFA PHC Project	~48 districts	$1,000,000	$0	Provide support for refresher training, M&E, and routine supervision of community health workers for appropriate use of RDTs and treatment with ACTs. PMI will support at least 10K CHWs.
	MAHEFA	~32 districts	$1,000,000	$0	
Support for Malaria Peace Corps Volunteers	New RFA PHC Project	Nationwide	$12,000	$0	Support to a third-year PCV to work on implementation of malaria interventions. Funding will support 2 PCVs one each nested with the MAHEFA and New RFP PHC projects. This will include housing, transport and equipment.
	MAHEFA	Nationwide	$12,000	$0	
Technical assistance to diagnostic activities	CDC/IAA	Nationwide	$12,000	$0	One TDY for CDC to provide technical support for RDT implementation at the community level.
Subtotal			$4,338,650	$2,302,650	
Pharmaceutical and Commodity Management					
Strengthen supply chain for malaria commodities to the community level	PSI	Nationwide	$300,000	$0	Ensure the continuous supply of malaria products to CHWs. Support will include the supervision of CHW re-supply points. Activity will be co-funded with other USAID funding streams.
Subtotal			$300,000	$300,000	
Treatment					
Technical assistance to support community case management	CDC/IAA	Nationwide	$12,000	$0	One CDC TDY to provide technical support for community case management of malaria.
Subtotal			$12,000	$0	

Activity	Implementer			Location	Description
Subtotal: Case Management		$4,650,650	$2,302,650		
		BCC			
Implementation of community-based malaria activities through integrated CCM interventions through NGOs/FBOs	New RFA PHC Project	$200,000	$0	~48 districts	Support for NGO/FBO grants to expand the implementation of community-based IEC/BCC interventions and integrated malaria messaging. Approximately 70% will be for interpersonal and 30% mass communication.
	MAHEFA	$100,000	$0	~32 districts	
BCC to create demand for malaria prevention and control commodities and health behaviors.	PSI	$150,000	$0	Nationwide	Support for malaria IEC/BCC activities to create demand for prevention and case management including LLINs, ACT promotion and early treatment-seeking behavior.
Support to malaria Peace Corps Volunteers	Peace Corps	$30,000	$0	Nationwide	PMI will continue to support a third-year PCV to coordinate work with other MVs and PCVs in Madagascar. Funding breakdown is $16k to support 1 PCV, including housing, transport and equipment, and $14k for malaria trainings for all PCVs.
Subtotal: IEC/BCC		**$480,000**	**$0**		
		Capacity Building			
Subtotal: Capacity Building		**$0**	**$0**		
		M&E			
Continue support for 15 fever sentinel sites of the fever surveillance system	IPM	$300,000	$0	Nationwide	Support 15 fever sites to monitor impact of program interventions on severe malaria. PMI will continue to work to transition the management of the FSS to MOH/IPM.
Support preparation for a large national household survey (MIS 2015)	TBD	$200,000	$0	Nationwide	Support diagnostics for the 2015 MDG survey, assuming it will occur on time: includes malaria specific biomarkers.
Technical assistance to support M&E activities	USAID	$0	$0	Nationwide	One USAID TDY to provide technical support for IMPACT Evaluation and M&E activities.

				One CDC TDY to provide technical support for evaluation, surveillance, M&E activities.
Technical assistance to support M&E activities	CDC/IAA	$12,000	Nationwide	
Subtotal: M&E		**$512,000**	**$0**	
Staffing and Administration				
In country staffing and administration costs	USAID	$618,400	Nationwide	Support for USAID annual staffing and administration costs.
In country staffing and administration costs	CDC/IAA	$500,000	Nationwide	Support for CDC annual staffing and administration costs.
Subtotal: Staffing and Administration		**$1,118,400**	**$0**	
GRAND TOTAL		**$25,920,000**	**$14,577,600**